Norwegians in Michigan

DISCOVERING THE PEOPLES OF MICHIGAN

Arthur W. Helweg, Russell M. Magnaghi, and Linwood H. Cousins, *Series Editors*

Ethnicity in Michigan: Issues and People
Jack Glazier and Arthur W. Helweg

African Americans in Michigan
Lewis Walker, Benjamin C. Wilson,
and Linwood H. Cousins

Albanians in Michigan
Frances Trix

Amish in Michigan
Gertrude Enders Huntington

Arab Americans in Michigan
Rosina J. Hassoun

Asian Indians in Michigan
Arthur W. Helweg

Belgians in Michigan
Bernard A. Cook

Chaldeans in Michigan
Mary C. Sengstock

Copts in Michigan
Eliot Dickinson

Cornish in Michigan
Russell M. Magnaghi

Dutch in Michigan
Larry ten Harmsel

Finns in Michigan
Gary Kaunonen

French Canadians in Michigan
John P. DuLong

Germans in Michigan
Jeremy W. Kilar

Greeks in Michigan
Stavros K. Frangos

Hungarians in Michigan
Éva V. Huseby-Darvas

Irish in Michigan
Seamus P. Metress and Eileen K. Metress

Italians in Michigan
Russell M. Magnaghi

Jews in Michigan
Judith Levin Cantor

Latinos in Michigan
David A. Badillo

Latvians in Michigan
Silvija D. Meija

Lithuanians in Michigan
Marius K. Grazulis

Mexicans and Mexican Americans in Michigan
Rudolph Valier Alvarado
and Sonya Yvette Alvarado

Norwegians in Michigan
Clifford Davidson

Poles in Michigan
Dennis Badaczewski

Scandinavians in Michigan
Jeffrey W. Hancks

Scots in Michigan
Alan T. Forrester

South Slavs in Michigan
Daniel Cetinich

Yankees in Michigan
Brian C. Wilson

Discovering the Peoples of Michigan is a series of publications examining the state's rich multicultural heritage. The series makes available an interesting, affordable, and varied collection of books that enables students and educated lay readers to explore Michigan's ethnic dynamics. A knowledge of the state's rapidly changing multicultural history has far-reaching implications for human relations, education, public policy, and planning. We believe that Discovering the Peoples of Michigan will enhance understanding of the unique contributions that diverse and often unrecognized communities have made to Michigan's history and culture.

Norwegians in Michigan

Clifford Davidson

Michigan State University Press

East Lansing

Michigan State University Press
East Lansing, Michigan 48823-5245

Printed and bound in the United States of America.

16   15   14   13   12   11   10   1   2   3   4   5   6   7   8   9   10

ISBN: 978-0-87013-878-2

LIBRARY OF CONGRESS CATALOGING-IN-PUBLICATION DATA
Davidson, Clifford.
Norwegians in Michigan / Clifford Davidson
p. cm. — (Discovering the peoples of Michigan)
Includes bibliographical references and index.
ISBN 978-0-87013-878-2 (pbk. : alk. paper) 1. Norwegians—Michigan. 2. Norwegian Americans—
Michigan. 3. Norwegian Americans—Michigan—Social life and customs. I. Title.
F575.S2D38 2010
977.4'0043982—dc22
2009031722

Cover design by Ariana Grabec-Dingman
Book design by Charlie Sharp, Sharp Des!gns, Lansing, Michigan
Cover art is the *City of Grand Haven* at dockside. Courtesy of the Michigan Maritime Museum, South Haven.

Michigan State University Press is a member of the Green Press Initiative and is
committed to developing and encouraging ecologically responsible publishing
practices. For more information about the Green Press Initiative and the use of
recycled paper in book publishing, please visit *www.greenpressinitiative.org*.

Visit Michigan State University Press on the World Wide Web at *www.msupress.msu.edu*

For Arthur W. Helweg, friend and scholar,
whose imagination and persistence brought into being
the series in which this book appears

ACKNOWLEDGMENTS

My greatest indebtedness is to Dennis Darling, who, along with his wife Jean, introduced me to the northwest coastal area of Michigan's Lower Peninsula and provided help in many ways, including graphics and photography. The members of the Askeladden Lodge of the Sons of Norway were incredibly enthusiastic, and I especially need to single out Inger Thoen, Louise Adams and her rosemaling group, Holly Jensen, Orlin and Helen Loen, and Donna Kaarlie, as well as those who provided Norwegian recipes. I also need to thank all of those from other Sons of Norway lodges in the state who helped with information and encouragement. Individuals who were of assistance are so numerous that it is not possible to name them all, but I feel obliged to mention Pauline Baver, Joseph Mihal, Elizabeth Melkild, Peter Sandman, Henry M. Yaple, Larry Syndergaard, James Nyquist, Rose Wolvert, Rae Holman, and Tom Krol, as well as the anonymous reader for the Press. Dennis Flessland, Norwegian consul in Michigan, kindly gave encouragement to the project. The Scandinavian hymnal collection of my dear late wife, Audrey Ekdahl Davidson, was of considerable usefulness in the consideration of the religion of Norwegian immigrants. Indispensable documents were made available by archivists at the Bentley Historical Library at the University of Michigan, the Norwegian-American Historical Association collection at St. Olaf College, the Michigan Maritime Museum, the Benzie Area Historical Museum, the Southwest Michigan Archives at Western Michigan University, and the Norwegian Lutheran Church Historical Society at Calumet, among others. It was a pleasure to work with the editorial staff of Michigan State University Press.

Contents

Introduction 1

Norwegians Come to Michigan 5
Michigan as a Transit Route and as Destination 13
Norwegian Sailors in Michigan Waters 17
Farming in the Lower Peninsula 27
Logging and the Lumber Industry 37
Norwegian Miners and Community in the "U.P." 41
Ishpeming and Skiing 47
Bridges, Tunnels, and Motorcars 51
Diversity of Gifts 57
The Religion of Norwegian Americans 67
The Music of Norwegian Americans 79
Arts and Crafts 85
Folklore, Superstitions, and Humor 95
Relief for German-Occupied Norway, 1940–45 103
Christmas and All the Trimmings 109

SIDEBARS

Car Ferry *Ann Arbor No. 4*, Sunk at Pier at Frankfort 21

A Sailors' Song 22

Harry B. Hanson, Engineer 54

David Frimodig, Forester and Local Historian 59

A Norwegian Nurse 63

Religion at Home 74

St. Olaf 76

The Hardanger Fiddle 81

Norwegian Repertoire 83

Knitting 90

Rosemaling 92

Askeladden 96

Jokes about Swedes 100

The Rev. Walter B. Scarvie, Head of Norwegian Relief in Michigan 106

A Christmas Carol 113

APPENDICES

Appendix 1. Martin Ulvestad's Survey of Norwegian Settlements
    in Michigan 117

Appendix 2. Norwegian Heritage 121

Appendix 3. Norwegian Hymns and Songs 125

Appendix 4. A Norwegian American's Memory of the Occupation 129

Appendix 5. Food 131

Notes 139

For Further Reference 149

Index 153

Introduction

Aside from Leif Eirikson and his men who came to the shores of North America in about 1000 C.E., perhaps landing at L'Anse aux Meadows in Newfoundland where Norse artifacts have been found, the first Norwegians to arrive were religious dissenters who made the voyage from Norway on the sloop *Restauration* in 1825. Settling in upper New York State, none of these went on to Michigan. A quarter of a century after the *Restauration*, there were still very few Norwegians in Michigan, but a quarter of a century later, their presence was beginning to be felt. Yet as an ethnic group, they never became dominant in Michigan, with many who live there in the early twenty-first century being part of an influx from other states, such as Minnesota, Iowa, and Illinois, rather than directly from Norway. The numbers of those with Norwegian ancestry is also enhanced by intermarriage, often but not at all exclusively with other Scandinavians.

Norway is a country that was regarded as exotic, on the northwest corner of the European world and with culture and values that certainly at first seemed strange and foreign to Americans, almost as if coming from the edge of the civilized world. The land not only has an immensely long border with Sweden but also touches Finland and Russia in the north, where the Sami people have a distinct culture of their own. It had extended contact and a not always happy relationship with Denmark, which affected its

*Norway, showing selected
counties, regions, and towns.*

language to a greater or lesser degree, depending on the region. Its dialects
were sufficiently diverse, due to the remoteness of much of the country, that
Norwegians from the southeast could understand Swedish (at least from the
southern provinces of Sweden) or Danish—but only with difficulty, or not at
all, the language of the people from the North along the Arctic Circle.

  In Michigan histories, it is no surprise that, due to their small numbers
and cultural prejudices on the part of the American population, Norwegians
received little attention. Yet they came, found their place in Michigan counties and towns, prospered, and contributed to the general economy. They
also contributed to the state's intellectual and cultural life, and they continue

to do so. Some families have disappeared into the American mainstream; others have resisted acculturation for various reasons. Some hardly know that they have Norwegian ancestors; some have nostalgia for the Old Country; some, on account of their emotional ties, prefer to consider themselves mainly to be part of the European diaspora; others identify with Norwegian ethnic organizations. Except for new arrivals, most have lost their ability to speak or read Norwegian.

No short book such as this can do justice to the entire subject of Norwegian immigration and the Norwegian presence in Michigan. The purpose of this little volume, nevertheless, is to illuminate aspects of the coming of Norwegians and their role in the state.

Norwegians Come to Michigan

The first Norwegians came as immigrants to the state in the middle of the nineteenth century, but not in the numbers that began to arrive in Wisconsin, Minnesota, and Iowa in those years. According to one accounting, the 1850 census reported only eighty-six native-born Norwegians in Michigan, and in 1890 there were nearly eight thousand in a state with two million residents. By 1910 more than 16,000 people who were either immigrants or of Norwegian ancestry were recorded, and this included those of "mixed" heritage, often involving intermarriage with Swedes.[1] The 2000 census gives a figure for Michigan of nearly 90,000 (out of 4.5 million people who claimed Norwegian ancestry nationally). These, of course, include many who came to the state from elsewhere in the United States to live in Michigan and contribute to its economy and cultural life.

However, it is also true that a Scandinavian, and specifically Norwegian, ancestry is much more widely present in Michigan than is commonly recognized, as also elsewhere throughout much of the United States. This is the case on account of long-ago historical factors: the famous Viking raids and settlements outside Scandinavian territories beginning in the late eighth century.[2] Following the brutal early incursions of Viking warriors, Norwegians especially came as farmers and traders to England, Scotland, and Ireland—as well as, along with Danes, to the Continent, even establishing

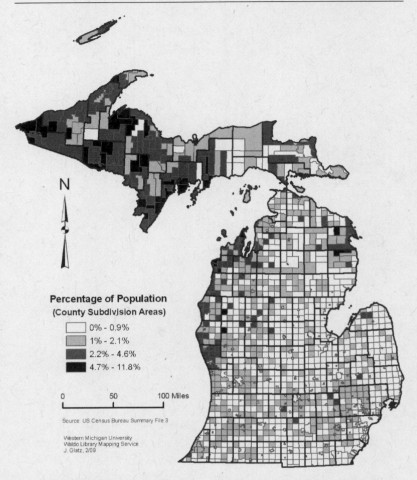

Population density map, showing percentage of persons claiming Norwegian ancestry,
U.S. Census, 2000.

footholds in southern Europe. In Northern England, Scotland, and nearby
islands, there are those who still trace their ancestry to Norway, even,
as folklore has it, claiming that an elongated toe—the toe next to the big
toe—is a sign of their descent from Vikings.[3] England for a time was even
ruled by a Nordic king, Canute. Prior to his reign, a large part of the country
had already been carved out in East Anglia and extending northward. The
city of York was the seat of Nordic kings, the last one being Eirik Bloodaxe
(d. 954). It should also be remembered that William the Conqueror, who

successfully invaded England in 1066, arrived on typical Viking ships from
Normandy, which had become a Scandinavian enclave from the time of
Rollo the Northman in 911 C.E. The eastern coast of Ireland likewise had
been dominated by the Norwegians, and Dublin had become a Norwegian
city and part of a power center that is sometimes called the Dublin-York
axis. Studies of the DNA of a sizable percentage, perhaps even a majority,
of Michigan residents, especially those with ancestors in parts of England,
Scotland, and Ireland, would thus inevitably show a strong connection to
Norwegian ancestors.

The new arrivals in Michigan from Norway in the nineteenth century,
then, were part of a second great explosion of Scandinavian emigration—
greater in numbers than during the Viking period, when the exodus led people to go to locations as far away as Iceland, Greenland, and Sicily—and even
to the coast of North America. While the Norwegian economy and poverty
were important reasons for this more recent surge of emigration, there was
also a psychological aspect: a serious dissatisfaction with life in Norway that
would be encouraged by enthusiastic reports from America. Letters from
America, some of them published in the Norwegian press, offered glowing
reports to those remaining in their home country. One such letter, written to
countrymen at Moss, offers something more than prosperity:

> We hope, dear countrymen, that you will not infer . . . that we bewail the day
> that we left our dear fatherland. No; do not misunderstand us; for we recall
> with gladness the day we left the chill cliffs of Norway and praise the Lord
> whose wisdom guided us so that our lot has been to dwell in a land where
> liberty and freedom prevail, for here we can enjoy all the privileges to which
> we are rightfully entitled.[4]

Another letter proclaimed the United States as the land of liberty:

> Here it is not asked, what or who was your father, but the question is, what
> are you? . . . It would be far from our purpose to rouse a spirit of discontent,
> but as American citizens who have tasted the joys of being free of the yoke
> of the tyrants . . . and having in common with you the Norwegian temper,
> love of liberty, and warmth of heart, we would say to you who dwell amid
> Norway's mountains: Show yourself worthy sons of the north.[5]

Other such letters also underlined the independence and the abundance, sometimes quite exaggerated, offered by the newfound land of America.

There is no doubt about the continuing demographic and economic crisis that nineteenth-century Norway was undergoing. In 1865, at the end of the American Civil War, the country had fewer than two million citizens. Within a period of just fifty years, Norwegian emigrants numbered 750,000, and yet the population of the country continued to rise, increasing to 2.5 million by World War I.[6] Changes in industry and farm organization also tended to impoverish many in small towns and villages as well as in the countryside, while the increased size of the population meant that there were simply more people than could be profitably sustained. If, for example, shoes now could be more efficiently produced and at a lower cost in factories, the local shoemaker was no longer able make a living. For brilliant young men not fortunate enough to be born into the ruling class, the hard life of a Norwegian fisherman might thus be less appealing than the promise of a better life in America. By law, property was passed on to the eldest son, and hence younger members of a family would be left without farms or small businesses that had been owned by their ancestors for generations.

There are still signs that serve as reminders of the burgeoning population. By the beginning of the nineteenth century in the parish church at Råde, in Østfold southeast of Christiania (now Oslo), additional seating had been required for the growing congregation. A large balcony was erected over the left part of the nave, very nearly doubling the available seating on that side, which conventionally was provided for women and children. Men sat on the right side. The additional space had thus been needed for the great increase in children, who sat with their mothers. As the young people of the parish grew to maturity, their prospects were much reduced from those of their parents, with local opportunities, here limited mainly to farming and fishing, not able to supply them with adequate jobs. This was particularly disconcerting in light of the growing disparity in wealth, with poverty more widespread and the affluent becoming arrogant in their relations with the less fortunate—an imposition of social distance that was highly resented. In response, some might sail before the mast on international waters, and others might need to accept menial work, when available. Yet those who emigrated often hoped to return to Norway when conditions improved or when they had made their fortunes abroad.

If people encountered hard times upon arrival in America, they still often felt that they were better off here than in the Old Country in spite of mixed feelings about leaving. Despite a nostalgia for home, their memories often tended to dwell on hard times in Norway. In one instance, a husband and wife had been employed in Norway by a well-to-do landowner, whose wife rationed the potatoes they were allowed to eat each day. To be sure, in the 1860s there were also crop failures, economic depression, and other pressures brought about, as we have seen, by technological change. On the farms there was a real fear of famine. A family legend has it that one spring there were only dried peas to eat, and everyone was thoroughly tired of them. The children would plunge their spoons upside down into the bowl of peas and say, "If you want to come, hang on." When a new supply was required by the household, the husband, who also despised this food, went to a farmer to buy another bushel of peas. He put his bushel basket upside down into the bin of peas, and said, "If you want to come, hang on."

Since Norway is now much richer per capita than the United States, it may be hard to understand the excitement of leaving home for a very difficult life abroad in a land that was essentially unknown except for reports from families, friends, and newspaper accounts, especially the famous "America letters" that, as we have seen, often painted an idealized portrait of life abroad. There was an emigration "fever" that even affected those who were very far from marginal people in Norway and who felt the beckoning of the New World. Though Michigan was not a major destination like Wisconsin or Minnesota, the state could offer work in the lumber camps and in mining, in the Great Lakes shipping, and through the opportunity to own farms.

Karl Birkeland, who was to change his name to Charles Barke, arrived in Michigan at age nineteen in 1872 from Sunnfjord, north of Bergen. As a younger son without hope of ever owning property in Norway, he had nevertheless learned the technicalities of sheep farming there. Following directions on a piece of paper, he came to the Oceana County farmhouse of Henry Hendrickson with a little scrap on which was written "Jeg kom til Hendrikson den 16 September." Four years later, he purchased his own farm with money borrowed toward a down payment of $300—and for the remaining $700 he indentured himself to an American, Ezra Scott. The initial debt was paid off in six years, but it would be another twelve years before he was entirely debt free.[7] Sheep were rare in Michigan at this time, and hence his background proved invaluable in providing a commodity both scarce locally and of value to his neighbors. Typically for a Norwegian farmer, he also diversified. He raised horses—a reminder that these animals were the main means of locomotion since the only public transportation on land at this time was provided by railroads.

It was in 1846 that Harriet Pierson came to a location that seems to have been northwest of Manistee, where her family immediately encountered extreme hardship as they prepared to establish a farm. First they "built a fire by the side of a tree, it being near night. The next thing we done we prepared our waggon and in it took lodging for the night." Without delay, on "the next day we built us a tent which we occupied for five days and five nights. During the meantime we built us a shanty which we now occupy." Brush had to be cleared before they could plant their crops of wheat, corn, and potatoes. In the first year they cleared seven acres and were looking forward to the founding of a school for the children, possibly in two years. "We are in the woods but I feel quite at home," she reported.[8] This, and other reports like it suggest the tremendous energy and hope brought by the Norwegian immigrants to their endeavors far away from their homeland.

Not surprisingly, the Norwegian immigrants brought with them an ambivalent attitude toward both their home country and their newfound land. At first they would cling tenaciously to their customs even as they enthusiastically embraced the new freedom of life in Michigan or the states on the other side of Lake Michigan. The more conservative-minded might consider progressive immigrants or their offspring to be subversive or even somewhat mad, and writers such as O. E. Rølvaag, though not writing about immigrants who settled in this state, saw the need to bridge the two cultures.[9] Some who came from the "Old Country" never stopped longing for "home," by which they meant their native towns, villages, or farms in Norway. It was not unusual for Norwegian immigrants to refuse to learn English, in which case they were listed in census reports as illiterate because they were unable to read or write the language of the country. Many of those who failed—or refused—to become American citizens nevertheless did not return "home." For these folk, expressions of flag-waving American patriotism—for example, when during World War I the governor of Iowa attempted to prohibit speaking in any language but English, even on the telephone—certainly seemed strangely threatening.[10] Naturally, they felt even more isolated and alienated when restrictions were put in place against immigration after the war. At the same time, younger Norwegian Americans tended more and more in the 1920s to embrace the English language and American customs. Ironically, it was a Norwegian American nurse, Theresa Erickson, who is credited with coining the patriotic slogan "One flag, one country, one language," which was introduced in the 1920s as a creed by the Americanization Committee of the Veterans of Foreign Wars.[11] Such could be the clash of cultures.

Michigan as a Transit Route and as Destination

The state never had the great influx of Norwegians experienced by the regions on the other side of Lake Michigan, but some of those who chose those more distant places nevertheless crossed its territory in earlier years. After 1850 a common route for immigrants interested in homesteading—the promise of cheap land to the west—was across the Lower Peninsula, with relatively few of these deciding to remain in the state. Even those who came through New York often went north on the Hudson River, then on to Buffalo to connect with the route by ship through Lake Erie to Detroit. One of the hazards along this route was communicated by an immigrant from Manistee County:

On the canal boat between New York and Buffalo we were visited by Pastor ———, who complained about the small size of our group. Nevertheless he wished to provide guidance for a few days and to care for us both physically and spiritually. He sang and prayed, and desired to know if we had money that was valid [in the United States]. He said (and it was true) that sometimes immigrants fell into the hands of publicans and sinners. A number of us showed our purses, which mainly held twenty-dollar gold coins. These, he said, were too large for use in Wisconsin [sic—Michigan], so he volunteered to exchange them for the current coinage. The next morning the "priest" and the gold coins had disappeared. Hence there was sorrow and anxiety among the poor immigrants who were now bereft of their much needed money.[12]

Unfortunately, such predators who would cheat and steal from immigrants as they traveled were all too common along the way. In later years, however, the route would change, and the train journey was chosen as the way across to Chicago and beyond. In this case, Norwegians coming to Michigan's Lower Peninsula would most likely come up from Chicago.

The voyage from Norway and the journey are described as remembered by Per Hansa's wife Beret in O. E. Rølvaag's *Giants in the Earth*, regarded as the most notable Norwegian American novel, published in translation after being initially issued in Oslo in 1924–25. First, she and her family, setting forth from northern Norway, sailed along the coast to Namsos, where they boarded a sailing vessel in which they would sail for many weeks. It was a dangerous passage in those days if a ship were unduly delayed by head winds or storms, and the accommodations on board were grim indeed. Food and water might be in short supply, and illnesses, lacking medical care, could be fatal. "At last," Beret remembers, "they had landed in Quebec," which, however, "was only the beginning of the real journey." In spite of her revolt against continuing, she did go on westward. "One fine day they had stood at Detroit, Michigan." But on she and her family must go. "Farther and farther onward . . . always west. . . . For a brief while there had been a chance to relax once more; they had travelled on water again, and she could hear the familiar splash of waves against the ship's side." It again was not a pleasant voyage across Lake Michigan, for there was "ill treatment" and "a great deal of bullying and brawling on board" before they arrived in Milwaukee. Then, of course, onward they must go—much farther, to the Dakota territories.[13] This fictional journey was one that was quite commonly taken by actual newcomers from Norway across the state of Michigan in about 1870, the time Rølvaag chose for his immigrants' arrival in the United States.

Per Hansa and his family would presumably have crossed Lake Michigan from the harbor at Grand Haven, at that time a port of call for sailing ships. Such vessels retained their importance for passenger service until after the Civil War. The route over Lake Michigan would be favored by many real-life immigrants coming through Detroit, especially after the railroad reached

Battle Creek in 1846. A letter from Johan Gasmann, captain of the ship *Salvator*, that was published in Norway in 1844 indicated that the construction of the rail line to Grand Haven was on schedule (he was overly optimistic), and that when finished, the time needed for travel would be two days less than by steamer to Chicago or Milwaukee. And it would be a much less strenuous journey across the state.[14] This route would, of course, be made more convenient when the rail line, operated by the Detroit, Grand Haven, and Milwaukee Railroad, was extended to Lake Michigan.

One immigrant who came by the Quebec–St. Lawrence–Detroit–Grand Haven route (and in 1866 brought eighty-two others, some of whom stayed in Michigan) was Ole Mathias Stubhaug, who had initially settled at Stony Creek.[15] For the majority of the immigrants who wished to cross Lake Michigan, steamship passenger transport had become available in 1858 and continued until World War I, when the Cross-Lake Ferry Line discontinued its service.[16] Well before 1917, Norwegian and other immigrants were entering through New York and traveling by rail through Chicago, even if their destination was Michigan.

Norwegian Sailors in Michigan Waters

The Lake Michigan crossing may have been favored in part during these early years because immigrants knew they would encounter Norwegians working the sailing boats and, later, the steamer service. Numerous Norwegians, seamen in their native land, settled along the Michigan, northern Illinois, Minnesota, and Wisconsin coasts to work on the boats. Indeed, it may be said from the available statistics that Norwegian sailors were the dominant ethnic group sailing as crews on the cargo and passenger ships of the Great Lakes, and a large number of officers were also Norwegian. These sailors came mainly from the south and west coasts of Norway.[17]

The lumber trade, to which we shall return later, was dependent on a large number of sailing ships to take boards from the sawmills to Chicago and Milwaukee. The first shipment of lumber destined for building the Chicago stockyards was carried on the *Dawn*, which was owned by John Oleson, who had been born at Egersund in 1839 and whose father had built the sloop *Restauration*, which, as we have seen, carried the first group of Norwegian immigrants to America in 1825.[18] Lumber was loaded at Traverse City, Ludington, Manistee, and other northern ports, but also at southern locations near rivers that transported logs downstream to the mills on the coast. This traffic could be quite profitable, and a captain such as Arthur N. Nelson, who had been born in 1845 at Larvik, could eventually become a

The City of Grand Haven *at dockside. The photo shows her after she was refitted as a schooner and clearly showing signs of old age. Wooden ships were considered old when they reached thirty years. This Michigan-built ship was of the workhorse type, on which Norwegian sailors sailed and carried lumber and other goods on Lake Michigan. Courtesy of the Michigan Maritime Museum, South Haven.*

ship owner. Christian M. Edwardson, born at Fredrikstad in 1857, had his residence, when not aboard the schooner of which he was part owner, first at Charlevoix and then at Manistee. In 1893 John L. Sørenson of Manistee owned the steam tug *Linderup*.[19]

Documentation is available for some of the ships of which Norwegians were officers. For example, the captain of the *City of Grand Haven* for a time was Hans Henry Pedersen.[20] This ship, built at Grand Haven and dating from 1872, had a wooden hull and a length of 127 feet. It was originally designed as a barge, but in 1884 it was fitted out with rigging and sails as a schooner. The *City of Grand Haven* would continue to serve in the lake trade until 1937. Less reliable is the report that the schooner *Melitta*, seventy feet in length, was rebuilt at Holland by Captain Abraham Anderson and Halvor Jensen.[21] Possibly, Anderson and Jensen only repaired the boat there, since official records do not indicate a full rebuilding at this location.

Michigan, famous for its lighthouses, was also served by such lighthouse tenders as the *Clover*, which under Captain Nils L. Larson, a native of Fredrikshald, was stationed at Sault St. Marie.[22] Lighthouses were, of course, essential for navigation on the lakes before modern technology since, as sailors

The schooner Melitta *under sail. She was smaller than the* City of Grand Haven, *but nevertheless carried a substantial load. Such ships sailed between Michigan ports and Chicago or Milwaukee. Ships of this class on which Norwegian sailors set out in Lake Michigan were quite different from modern pleasure boats or racing craft. Courtesy of the Michigan Maritime Museum.*

reported, storms in some seasons reminded them of the worst weather on the North Sea. A very large number of shipwrecks was recorded. Peter Peterson, lighthouse keeper at Escanaba, was able to save the crew of an English ship, for which the English government awarded him a gold medal.[23]

In November 1913, a storm that lasted four days struck the Great Lakes, with considerable loss of life and immense damage to shipping. In Lake Huron, the first mate was H. C. Hansen, who described how the heavy weather caused the steamship *D.O. Mills* nearly to be lost. Heading on its way from Buffalo to Duluth, the ship "was blown on the rocky shore at Harbor Beach, so high that there were only twelve feet of water where it was left standing. . . . The only thing that saved us was that we were thrown so high upon the beach."[24]

One fleet of steam-powered ships seemed to be particularly plagued with bad luck. These were the ferries that carried the cars of the Ann Arbor Railroad across Lake Michigan from Frankfort, which had a very good harbor that had been used in the lumber trade. Stabilizing railroad cars was difficult, and the earlier ferries were not even provided with sea gates to protect the stern from the waves. *Ann Arbor No. 4*, built at Cleveland in 1906, at least was fitted with a wooden sea gate. But on Valentine's Day in 1923, the flimsy sea gate provided little protection from the fury of a Lake Michigan storm. Its captain at this time was the Norwegian American Charles Frederickson, who, along with her heroic engineer, put up a valiant battle to save the ship in an 80-mile-per-hour gale that blew up shortly after they had departed from Frankfort. The temperature was -20° F. The ship was carrying automobiles as well as railroad cars, and the cargo broke loose. Around 2:30 A.M., with the sea gate now broken, the automobiles and one railroad car fell out from over the stern, over which two coal cars became literally suspended. Another coal car fell through to the engine room, and one of its wheels pressed against the release valve on the pressure cylinder, "sliding up and down as [the ship] rolled."[25] Waves were crashing across the ship, which was taking on water dangerously. Rails on deck were torn away, and even the whistle was broken. The smoke stack became loose. Visibility on account of the fog was only about a single boat length.

Captain Frederickson "seemed to be everywhere." With pipe in mouth, he came into the galley where some cold, hungry sailors were congregated. Some had wounds and even broken bones. "Boys," he said, "I have taken you to sea for a good many years, always bringing you safely home, and will do it this time if only you will give us a badly needed hand." He and his crew struggled to return the ship to Frankfort. At 7:00 A.M., *Ann Arbor No. 4*, already settling in the water, was making an approach to the south pierhead when a wave smashed down on her and she hit the pier. She began to list sharply, but Captain Frederickson, true to his Scandinavian sense of duty, did not want to leave his command. He laconically said, "She has been a faithful old girl, bringing us all back home, so I guess I will stick around and see how she lays her."[26] He was angry at being dragged off to safety as the ship sank in twenty-two feet of water. There was no loss of life, in spite of the

The car ferry Ann Arbor No. 4, *sunk at the pier at Frankfort after the Valentine's Day storm in February 1923. Photo courtesy of the Benzie Area Historical Museum.*

Car Ferry *Ann Arbor No. 4*, Sunk at Pier at Frankfort

The 1923 Valentine's Day storm seems to have been one of the more violent of the century on Lake Michigan. Captain Frederickson and his crew, which included other Norwegians such as second mate O. B. Olsen, successfully fought against the elements to keep her afloat until they reached port.

The car ferries, which sailed throughout the winter months, were particularly vulnerable. *Ann Arbor No. 4* had come close to disaster more than once previously—for example, in February 1912, when she was commanded by Captain Alexander Larson, she was caught in a dangerous ice floe near Manistique. Even in good weather, such ships could come to grief. In May 1909, *No. 4*, carrying iron ore, had previously capsized in the Manistique harbor.*

* Arthur C. Fredrickson, and Lucy F. Fredrickson, *Fredrickson's History of the Ann Arbor Auto and Train Ferries* (Frankfort, MI: Gulls Nest, 1994), 51–53, 61, 100–105.

injuries suffered by the engineer and others, and the ship itself was repaired and returned to service.

The Ann Arbor ferries were large, but not as large as other ships on the Great Lakes that were commanded by Norwegians or men of Norwegian descent. A. S. Carlsen of Menominee was captain of the steamer *Cletus*

A Sailors' Song

Singing at such events as *Syttende Mai* or the Fourth of July might include patriotic songs, but also nostalgic melodies of the Old Country such as "Hils fra meg der hjemme"—a sailors' song, but a favorite of all immigrants who still longed for Norway as their true home. Sometimes grown and hardened fishermen cried when this song was sung,* for Norwegians often felt they were aliens and strangers in the New World. "Home" was Norway, even for those who had lived most of their lives in America.

(Chorus):

Hils fra meg der hjemme	Greet those who are at home,
Hils min far og mor,	Greet my father and mother,
Hils de grønne lier	Greet the green hillsides
Og den blanke fjord.	And the glittering fjord.
Hvis jeg hadde vinger	If I had wings
Fløy jeg hjem med deg	I would fly home to you.
Til de lyse netter.	To the luminous nights
Hils dem! Hils fra meg.	Greet them! Greet them from me.

Schneider, an ore boat, in the 1920s. O. A. Johnson was captain of the *Henry Ford II* in 1928; this massive steel-hulled ship, built in 1924 for the Ford Motor Co., was almost six hundred feet in length and sixty-two wide, with a depth of twenty-seven feet.[27]

Sailors were not always employed in shipping. Other Norwegian immigrants, accustomed to the sea, turned to fishing, sometimes from small boats operating even in the coldest parts of Lake Superior. Life could be very isolated, but no more so than in the fishing communities that existed for a century on Isle Royale, until it became a national park and fishing was depleted by invasive species, lamprey eels and smelt. Immigrants from Nordland (northern Norway) had been attracted here in the middle of the nineteenth century—folk who were reported to be uncommunicative but friendly.[28] Even in the early twentieth century, Isle Royale and the many smaller islands that surrounded it were regularly connected to the mainland

(Verse):

I den stille tause natt,	*On the deck I stand at night*
Står jeg her ved skipets ratt,	*When the stars above are bright,*
Under himlens stjernevell,	*Far away from friends and home,*
Ene og forlatt.	*Lonely here I roam.*
Under himlens høye tak	*Swallows on their wings so high,*
Høres fjerne vingeslag,	*Now in spring they homeward fly*
Fugletrekket atter går	*To the land where sunlight beams*
Mot nord, mot lyse vår.	*Into my childhood dreams.*[†]

(Repeat chorus).

Other Norwegian American favorites might include "Nikolina," a sentimental love song, which was sung and played in different versions, as would be typical of the oral tradition.[‡]

---

* Howard Sivertson, *Once upon an Isle: The Story of Fishing Families on Isle Royale* (Mount Horeb, WI: Wisconsin Folk Museum, 1992), 61.
† Norwegian text and translation (altered) from LeRoy Larson, "Scandinavian-American Folk Dance Music of the Norwegians in Minnesota," (Ph.D. diss., University of Minnesota, 1975), 2:19. The song was originally Swedish and entitled "Hälsa dem där hemma"; sometimes Norwegians sang the Swedish text.
‡ Larson, "Scandinavian-American Folk Dance Music," 1:106.

only by the arrival of the steamer *America*, succeeded by the *Winyah*.[29] The fish caught in Lake Superior, either by nets or trolling, had to be boxed and loaded from small boats onto the ship to Duluth, where in 1923 the price paid was eleven cents per pound.[30] Travel to lower Michigan would require a voyage to Minnesota and train through Chicago. Fortunately, the Norwegian fishermen and their families were unusually healthy,[31] since professional medical care on the island was unavailable, but life nevertheless was precarious in this northernmost reach of Michigan, where the lake could become treacherous without warning—especially when men ventured forth in small rowboats, as was the practice. Deaths, of course, did occur, but when it was not someone lost at sea, the preferred burial was normally on the mainland. The body would be packed in ice and shipped by steamer to Duluth.[32]

For those who stayed over the winters, the isolation was even more acute since the lake would be impassible, and during this period the fishermen would turn to trapping. When steamer passage resumed in the spring, the furs would be marketed at Duluth. A close view of conditions during the bitterly cold winters is provided by Dorothy Simonson, who spent one season there as a schoolteacher living in the Holger and Lucy Johnson household in proximity to Chippewa Harbor.[33] The winter was in full force from early December, and heating was by means of an inefficient stove, for which wood had to be carried in from out of doors. With no running water or plumbing, family members used chamber pots, which had to be emptied. Floors were cold. Lighting was with kerosene lamps, but in this year fuel was all used up by April 5. Vegetables were nearly gone by the end of February, except for potatoes. Coffee, especially loved by Norwegians, and also butter were in short supply. Moose, nevertheless, seemed to be everywhere and were a source of protein for the families. Fortunately, when Ms. Simonson was resident on the island, radio transmission had been established, though by present-day standards the equipment was primitive and required a working generator to keep batteries charged. In spite of having been educated at Northern State Teachers College (now Northern Michigan University), this energetic woman, who was paid only $65 per month, from which she paid $35 for board, clearly found the hardship of winter on the island a shock.

There was no church on Isle Royale. The people there were conventionally religious, and some arranged Bible classes for their children, remembered Howard Sivertson, whose grandparents had arrived from Egersund in 1892.[34] Prayers before meals were normal in Norwegian families elsewhere at that time, and very likely here as well. In the spring and summer, two festivals were celebrated: *Syttende Mai* (the Seventeenth of May, which is Norwegian Constitution Day) and the Fourth of July. Families would gather, and on the latter a picnic and perhaps a ball game would be normal.[35] Elling Seglem, who spent summers on the island, reported that on July 4, 1932, fishermen, their families, and some tourists gathered, at first going to Hay Bay and then Malone Island, afterward to Holger Johnson's dock at Chippewa Harbor, where the list of those present included such names as Sivert Anderson, Ed Kvalvik, Albert Bjorvek, Ed Ronning, and Mr. Benson. There was music and dancing, as would have been the case in Norway, and, as Seglem said, "plenty of home brew and a barrel of fun." A fight broke out as well. When Holger Johnson's wife attempted to intervene in the fight, which involved a

Swede from Småland (presumably a hired man), she was knocked down and given a black eye.[36]

Singing at such events might include patriotic songs but also nostalgic melodies of the Old Country such as *Hils fra meg der hjemme*, a sailors' song but a favorite of all immigrants who still longed for Norway as their true home. On Isle Royale, as in other Norwegian fishing communities, the next day would mean a return to work, with boys engaged along with their fathers and girls assisting their mothers, whose household labors involved much more than the modern housewife's tasks. Nets had to be mended—again women's work. For the men, boats required looking after, and of course there was the constant need to put out to sea to do the actual work of fishing. Among all their other tasks, women had to make all their own clothes—even underwear. And before the arrival of the sewing machine, every stitch had to be done by hand. But recreation was not neglected in a normal week.[37] On Friday nights, members of the community would gather for card games.[38]

Farming in the Lower Peninsula

For the Norwegians who took up agriculture, their choice was often to locate in the northwestern counties, usually where there were other options for seasonal employment. Almost all of those who came were not city dwellers, and the men were used to combining farming with such endeavors as fishing or seafaring. Many locations in this area of the state too would have reminded them of their native Norway—the terrain, the vegetation, the proximity to a large body of water. The land was suitable for orchards and mixed livestock, including mainly cows, chickens, and hogs. Farms were small and suited to subsistence agriculture. Immigrants could be grouped closely enough together to feel very much part of a community and often had come from a particular region in Norway, sometimes being acquainted before leaving their native country. Some had been persuaded to emigrate by letters sent back to them from their friends in America. They were knowledgeable in advance from their Norwegian experience about how to build log houses and clear the land for tilling. This was not open prairie, and hence the work of clearing the land with primitive equipment (an axe, a chain to hitch around tree stumps) and horses was backbreaking. Fortunately the immigrants were very much work oriented. Alternative occupations that could assist them in acquiring needed supplementary income were at hand, especially in logging, work in sawmills, fishing, and

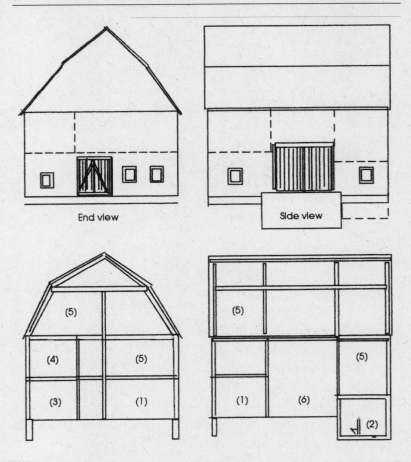

Cross-sectional views of typical Norwegian American farmstead barn at Elberta. This building housed (1) horses, (2) milk cows, (3) feed storage, (4) granary, (5) hay and straw lofts, and (6) some farm equipment in drive-in area. A site plan showing the location of buildings on this farmstead appears on the following page.

sailing. While they were away at such work, the women of the family took care of the farm, as they had done in Norway.

Sometimes immigrants originally planned to go on to Minnesota, Wisconsin, or Iowa. Peter Peterson and his wife Martha became confused at Chicago and ended up near Manistee, but liked the territory, where they remained—eventually celebrating their fiftieth wedding anniversary there. Photographs in the Norwegian American archives at Northfield show them

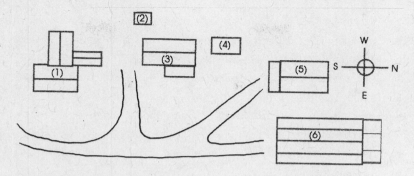

Site plan of Sivert Baver farm, in Benzie County. Several buildings on the farm had multiple uses. The house (1), which generally was home for an extended family, was much more than living quarters, for it was a center of food preparation (e.g., butter, canned goods). The necessary outhouse (2) was considered to be luxurious for such a structure and had a window. One building (3) contained a workshop, a smokehouse and meat storage area above, an ice house, and a woodshed. The chicken coop (4) was a separate building on skids that could be moved. The machine shed (5) housed tools for machine repairs; farm implements such as a mower, rake, and manure spreader; and overhead, a sleigh. A pig pen was located under the north end of the shed, and a corn crib was attached to it at the south. The barn (6) generally held four horses and up to ten milk cows as well as an area for calves and young stock. Scale drawing by Dennis Darling.

standing by their automobile in 1928, with a team and mower, and with horses and a load of hay by their barn. Another photo, after the family patriarch had passed away, shows four generations of the family.[39]

The most important building on the family farm was the barn, which could be arranged to accommodate cows, usually below a hay loft, as well as horses and sometimes chickens—though ideally the latter, like the hogs, would have their own sheds. Cream, which would be used to make butter, had to be separated from the milk by means of a cream separator, a Scandinavian invention introduced in 1877. Milk might be shared with the barn cats, considered valuable for control of rats and mice. Lofts were arranged so that the hay could be pulled directly and efficiently up from hay wagons into them by means of slings, and in the following winter it could be pitched down a chute directly to the animals. When in the barn, cows were locked in wooden stanchions that allowed them to stand or lie down but not move about in the barn. This helped to maintain cleanliness since their waste would be dropped conveniently into a gutter behind them; from this it was easily scooped out daily using a manure fork and taken to the manure pile, usually in a wheelbarrow. However, the cows were allowed exercise whenever possible, both day and night in the summer. Only in the coldest or stormiest weather was it necessary to keep the cows inside for twenty-four hours a day. An important aspect of the layout of the farm was the location of the well, which needed to be convenient to the barn in order to provide a supply of water for cows and horses. Those who were lucky or sufficiently well-off would acquire windmills to draw the water so that it would not have to be pumped by hand.

Since the earliest Norwegian settlers arrived with few means, they initially would have only a few animals and little equipment. At first, hay and oats for the animals usually had to be harvested manually with a scythe, which in turn needed frequent sharpening. For this, a large grindstone wheel, turned either with a crank or by means of pedals, was used. Grains required that a cradle be attached to the scythe so that the stalks could be collected and bound in bundles. Even with the advent of the first reapers, bundling still had to be done by hand. Children, often very young, were employed in this work.[40] After the introduction of a new type of grain reaper, the "self-binder," in the 1870s, the bundles still had to be picked up and set upright in shocks of (usually) nine bundles—three on each side, one on each end, and one on top—to dry before threshing. With the arrival of the threshing rig, farmers traded their labor so as to organize sufficient crews to dismantle the shocks of grain, pitch them onto farm wagons, and bring them to the machine, in early years powered by a steam tractor. The straw would be used for bedding under the cattle and horses, and the grain itself was stored in a granary. Some of the grain would necessarily be retained for planting the next year's new crop, again a labor-intensive procedure until the development of the "drill," or mechanical seeder, which of course was initially horse drawn. Fields were fertilized with compost derived from manure from the farm animals, at first spread by hand from wagons and then eventually by mechanical manure spreaders. Using natural organic fertilizer and crop rotation, farmers achieved sustainable and ecologically superior agriculture, though on a small scale compared to many of today's farms.

One profitable crop, potatoes, was not mechanized. After the fields had been prepared by plowing and disking or harrowing, the spuds had to be placed in the ground by hand in furrows with the "eyes" facing upward.

A Norwegian American farmer harvesting corn with a corn binder, a machine developed after the design of the "self-binder" for grains such as oats, barley, and wheat. This machine is late nineteenth-century in date, and the John Deere tractor is a mid-1930s model. It was common for frugal Norwegian-American farmers to use antiquated machinery as long as possible before replacing it with more up-to-date equipment. The photograph dates from the 1940s. Photo: Collection of the author.

Prior to the development of DDT, potato bugs were reported in some cases to have been controlled by an arsenic spray. Corn could be planted by hand with a simple device, but by the beginning of the twentieth century this was replaced by horse-drawn corn planters. Other equipment also became available as well, so that by the beginning of World War I, most farms of Norwegian immigrants were able to have a considerable assortment of machinery, which might include hay loaders that would gather the hay from long windrows and deposit it on horse-drawn hay wagons to be taken to the barn or pitched onto haystacks. Tractors would follow as necessary equipment in the 1920s and 1930s.

Norwegian American descendants report that the difference in life between the early days and the present might best be gauged not only by the quiet enveloping the farm, not yet punctuated by the sounds of tractors or engines on water pumps or saw rigs, but also by the darkness that spread out over it at night. Rural electrification was only effected by the New Deal in the years immediately before World War II. Kerosene lanterns were used by farmers when milking their cows in the morning and evening on dark winter days; and in houses after sunset, some were lucky enough to have

Aladdin lamps, which produced slightly more illumination. Imagine what it was like for a child to do his or her homework during the school year in what would now be considered woefully inadequate lighting while wrapped in heavy clothing against the cold! Wood stoves could be woefully inefficient on frigid nights. Eventually many were able to afford furnaces, which might still, however, be wood-burning.

Initially the cramped quarters offered by a log house were typical. Anyone who has seen traditional log houses in Norway—as, for example, at the Norwegian Folk Museum on Bygdøy, near Oslo—will at once see the similarities between these and the structures built by Norwegian Americans.[41] Dovetailed joining was used in both cases. The second story was not of full height and was used as sleeping quarters. The two differences that have been noted are the use of whitewash and, in some cases, a kitchen addition set at right angles to the house.[42]

However, when in 1880 Iver Melkild came from Battenfjordsora, he had the unusual opportunity to purchase a log house that had already been built from the owner, the local Chippewa chief whose name was Peter Ringnose. He moved his house to the forty acres of farmland that he had acquired near Northport. In size it was 20 by 17 feet, essentially a one-room cabin with the kitchen area behind a partition at the rear. An overhead loft, which had to be entered by means of a ladder, was used for sleeping quarters. An apple orchard was planted near the cabin, but Iver's main income seems to have come from work on the car ferries on Lake Michigan, until his death in this line of work in 1907, when he was swept overboard.[43]

Iver's son Martin, who had worked when younger as a lumberman, married a widow, Inga, whose father had immigrated from Hegre in the Trondheim region. They purchased a sixty-acre farm near Northport where they grew apples, and she was employed as Leelanau Township librarian. The family history lists twenty varieties of apples, including Northern Spies, Duchess, Belmont, Seek-No-Further, and Golden Pippin, that were grown there. Apples as well as cider from this farm and from others nearby were packed in barrels and then shipped to market in Illinois and Wisconsin. Farmers typically complained about the low prices they were forced to accept from middlemen who purchased their apples and other commodities for resale in Chicago, Milwaukee, and other cities.[44] However, during the Great Depression of the late 1920s and 1930s, the family considered itself well-off since they had cows, chickens, and pigs. Farm products such as eggs, butter, and milk could be bartered for other necessities. They also had horses, which in those days were more economical than tractors and a better means of transport in the wintertime. The grain binder for harvesting oats for the animals was consequently still pulled by horses, while a steam-powered threshing machine was used until the modern tractor became available.[45]

The acquisition of a farm in Michigan was not as easy for immigrants as it was for those who settled in the lands to the west, where land was offered cheaply to homesteaders. In the fall of 1888, Peder Baver (Norwegian: Baevre) and his wife Marit arrived in America and located near present-day Elberta after selling their goods at auction at his farm in the Surnadal district not far from Kristiansund.[46] Their struggles must be seen as not untypical of the determination with which so many newly arrived Norwegians applied themselves. In spite of being considered well-to-do in Norway, they could only afford to bring five of their children—Eli, Ole, Sivert, Ole (Willy), and Margrethe, the latter only nine months old—with them, even though they economized by traveling in steerage. Two remaining girls, Synnøve (Susie) and Marit (Mary), would stay in Norway for two more years. Arriving in the fall, the family spent the winter on the Leonard Classen farm, where they stayed while Peder worked in a local sawmill. One daughter worked for a family of wealthy sawmill owners, the Cranes, for $1.50 a week. Two other daughters would later also work for the Cranes. Another child, Pettrina, would be born in the spring, by which time they had been able to afford to have their own house in Elberta.

The move to their farm had to wait until after yet another move and then the opportunity to obtain some timberland a few miles from Elberta from Classens and Glaerum, the previous owners, in exchange for logging it. To this Peder added another eighty acres, on which he built a house with an attached barn, and began farming at last—though of necessity for a time still working in the lumber camp, where his wife Marit also worked as a cook. Timber had to be cut on this land too, and it needed to be cleared of underbrush before serious farming could begin. Lumbermen assisted and actually lived for some years in the barn. A true farmhouse, which still exists, thus also needed to be built, and a cherry orchard was planted near it.

Peder, also possessing skills as a carpenter, turned them to good use—some of his creations are still prized family possessions—and Marit in turn carded wool from the sheep on their farm, spun yarn, and wove fabric. In 1910 their son Sivert bought the farm and purchased seventy more acres. After his marriage in 1913, he built an apartment onto the farmhouse for his parents, who lived there for the remainder of their long lives. Together father and son had dairy cattle and sold cream and butter commercially. Pauline, the eldest daughter of Sivert and his wife Anna, well remembers churning butter in the large churn in the basement under her mother's watchful eyes, and this would be packed in two-, four-, or five-pound crocks, which would be taken to town, in winter by a sleigh, to be delivered by her to customers.

Norwegians had learned how to diversify their produce to insure against the kind of failure to which single-crop farms are subject nowadays. Other produce from the Baver farm included potatoes, oats, and rye. In the 1920s, the orchards were expanded to include apple, peach, and plum trees. Raspberries too were grown and shipped to Chicago by boat to be sold.

A family history by Olga Wagbo, completed in 1982, gives another valuable picture of an immigrant family, in this case settling at East Jordan, located south of Charlevoix, with the plan of taking up farming.[47] At first, water had to be carried from a creek five hundred feet distant for both livestock and people. The log house would be replaced by a frame structure, again heated by a wood-burning stove. Cook stoves also used wood and had attached reservoirs that provided warm water for dishwashing, washing up, and bathing, the latter infrequent among early Norwegian Americans. On the whole, over the years farmers would be better off than those who merely worked for wages, and this was the case too because of the participation of women in the work that sustained the family. They would do knitting and dyeing, weaving, quilting, baking, tending vegetable gardens—even having a role in butchering. In the warm days of summer, the only available meat they could provide for the menfolk often consisted of pork preserved in salt brine. But they made jellies and picked fruit and wild berries. During the Depression, a neighbor, Lois Rude's mother, is said to have raised chickens, which were raided by red foxes.

There were other dangers. Martha Wagbo remembered a fire in June 1933 when a crack in the chimney set fire to their house. Such conflagrations had to be fought by the owners, who in this case threw all that they could out the windows. Fire trucks did not venture forth into the countryside in those days, and in any case, telephone service was either primitive or nonexistent.

Martha's mother rescued a setting hen from the basement, and a rhubarb pie was saved. "Well," a member of the family said, "we will have rhubarb pie for supper." A neighbor's house burned the next winter.

The establishment of a church was a high priority, and early in the century, a pastor would come once each month and stay with local farm families. The East Jordan Evangelical Lutheran Church was then founded in 1905, and the first pastor was John Maakestad, who arrived by horse team. The disused Episcopal church was rented, then a new structure was constructed five years later. After 1917, two services were held, one in Norwegian and one in English, led by the Rev. John Johnson, who stayed for more than thirty years. Norwegian services, however, had been abandoned at East Jordan by 1925.

Like the Melkild children, the Wagbo youngsters were taken to school before World War II in a horse-drawn vehicle. It was through their education that they found entrance into the larger world. The family's descendants were lawyers, artists, barbers, and foresters, and they became scattered in other parts of the country—part of the assimilation of Norwegian Americans into the mainstream of America, but also a sign of the breakdown of the tightly knit rural community to which Norwegians had been accustomed.

In earlier times, Norwegian American women had undoubtedly formed the glue that linked the family, church, and community together. Women did far more than prepare church dinners, for which the Lutheran churches were famous. They cared for the children until they were old enough to work, which might be at ten years of age or younger, and were responsible for the many tasks involved in running the household. This would involve making their own soap; washing clothes, including baby diapers, in tubs (and boiling heavily soiled clothes on the stove); and seeing to the preservation of fruits and vegetables needed for the winter. Apples were kept in a cool place until well into the winter, albeit not always in perfect condition. Potatoes, beets, and carrots were stored in cellars. Eventually, with the introduction of home canning, they were able to add substantially to their family's diet. They were the ones who churned the butter and assisted at the slaughter of animals. They saw that their menfolk and children were well fed, albeit sometimes lacking in the nutritional balance that is recommended today.

Logging and the Lumber Industry

The forests of the northern and western parts of the Lower Peninsula fed the voracious appetite for lumber with which the great cities of Chicago and Milwaukee were built. Later, lumber would be needed for the building of Detroit as well, but not from this region of the state. Wood was also used in the Grand Rapids furniture factories and for shipbuilding at Bay City, Port Huron, and Grand Haven. While the loggers at first tended to be native born, as time went on, Scandinavians and other immigrants entered the ranks of the work force in this industry in considerable numbers. At the end of the century, much of the virgin timber was cut down, and by about 1912, more than 400 million feet of lumber had, for example, been taken from the remaining watershed of the Manistee River. The lumber boom, which had experienced its ups and downs over the years, was entirely finished by 1920 in the Upper Peninsula as well.

The Norwegians who were employed in the logging camps endured conditions that would never be tolerated today. Trees, if they were to be suitable, had to be cut in the wintertime, which could be brutally cold. Temperatures in some camps frequently dropped to -30° F or below. The men slept on bunk beds barracks-style in primitive cabins. One man complained about the "professional snorers from Germany, Norway, etc." who kept him awake.[48] The cookhouse had benches and long tables at which the men sat. The diet was far from balanced, and the drinking water was not boiled. Breakfast usually consisted of pancakes and coffee, dinner or supper possibly an unappetizing stew. Generally, sanitary conditions were deplorable. Logging crews would involve usually about fifty or sixty men. They had to provide and care for their own tools—peaveys (sometimes called cant hooks), axes, saws, and rope and tackle. The peaveys, wooden-handled tools with a sharp metal point and a hinged hook, were used to roll the extremely heavy logs, which had been cut into sixteen-foot lengths. Special large-wheeled horse-drawn carriages that could lift logs out of swampy areas—the logs were chained under the axles—were utilized, and thereafter, pulley systems powered by horses were adapted to raise them onto whatever carriage was being used for transport. Horses were also used for pulling the logs on sleds out of the forests, whereupon the logs were usually sent by water, in rivers and streams, to ports or to where a connection might be made to a railroad. When narrow-gauge rail was constructed, the men would be required to lay the ties and maintain the tracks only as long as they were needed.[49] Wages might be as low as a dollar a day,[50] while the lumber barons grew rich and could afford spacious and impressive houses such as those still standing in Traverse City and other lumber towns.

By 1855 legislation was passed to regulate the transfer of logs by water, including "booming and rafting." The logs were branded with their owners' marks, then sent downriver to holding booms—in effect, a dam through which they were sorted.[51] Rafts of logs then would be lashed together and transferred downriver to the sawmills. Muskegon alone had twenty-six saw-mills operating in the 1870s. This work too was dangerous, though it allowed the workers to live at home in towns or on their farms. After about 1875, steam engine–powered circular saws were introduced to cut the wood into lumber, and great piles of sawdust rose near them.[52] Planing mills as well as sawmills devoted to cutting cedar shingles were also part of the operation at Frankfort.[53] Lumber and shingles were to be seen stacked all around for drying and curing, or simply waiting to be shipped out. The location of the sawmills was important, since they needed to be conveniently located in order to facilitate loading onto sailing ships so the lumber could be to taken to the markets, mainly in the large and growing cities.

On Saturday night, the loggers and lumbermen were turned loose on the town. In Bay City, a four-block section known as "the Catacombs" was

Norwegian American Sivert Baver on left, with another logger, near Elberta. The large tree trunk shows the large size of the first-growth timber that was cut in the area. Early photograph courtesy of Pauline Baver.

particularly lawless, with sixty-five saloons or other establishments that sold alcohol.[54] Saloons had "pretty waiter girls," cited as prostitutes "of the most depraved and unscrupulous class."[55] Their price was between fifty cents and five dollars. In East Saginaw, the 1880 census reported thirty-two houses of prostitution, but in this town there were few Norwegians to be tempted.[56] Things seem to have been much more civilized in Muskegon, where there was a sizable Norwegian population. Peter Jensen and John Anderson operated the Dynamite Saloon on Ottawa Street, and in spite of the amount of alcohol said to have been consumed, their establishment had a reputation for maintaining strict order among its clientele.[57] Symptomatic too, perhaps, was the establishment in Muskegon County of five Norwegian Lutheran congregations, beginning with the First Evangelical Lutheran Church, but also including Norwegian Methodist and Baptist congregations before the end of the century.[58]

In Muskegon, the sizable population of Norwegian immigrants, who had started coming to the town in 1848, included sailors as well as lumbermen. They tended to settle along the lakefront on Jackson Hill, sometimes formerly known as Norwegian Hill, or Killgrubbin.[59] The high point of the lumber industry, and consequently of lake shipping, was in the 1880s. The

Muskegon Booming Company delivered 570,552,791 feet of logs to the mills in 1887. The business then suddenly collapsed with the market crash and panic of 1890, which ushered in hard times that were long remembered by Norwegian Americans.[60]

Another effect of the lumber boom was the widespread clear-cutting of timber that more or less devastated the countryside, with resulting erosion and widespread forest fires that threatened the entire western part of Michigan.[61] Foresters and ecologists have long considered the waste and depredation of the state's forests to have been one of the great scandals suffered in Michigan's history, and of course proof also of the danger of unregulated capitalism, which made a few families rich and provided few benefits or protections for the workers. If Norwegians and others of so many different nationalities had provided the material for the building of great American cities, the cost to the state's natural resources was nevertheless immense.

Norwegian Miners and Community in the "U.P."

In the Upper Peninsula, the discovery of rich deposits of copper in the far north of the state in the Keweenaw Peninsula immediately prior to the Civil War would precipitate an influx of Europeans who came to work in the mines. Laborers, recruited abroad from a range of nationalities, were lured to the region with the promise that they would have jobs and be exempt from service in the Union Army. (Copper was a commodity that was vital for the war effort.)[62] Work in the mines was dangerous and unpleasant, with the shafts in which the miners worked extending deep underground. Access was down a series of long, steep ladders resting on successive platforms. In the deep darkness of the mines, light was cast by candles fixed on the miners' helmets. The labor was difficult, the pay known to be poor, the chance of injury and death great.[63] Miners' clothes were almost immediately stained the color of copper. A description of the Cliff Mine at Clifton by a schoolteacher in 1863 gives a grim picture. The mines were damp. Shafts might penetrate more than a mile below the surface. Since they extended below the water table, water constantly had to be pumped out. Loosening the copper from the shaft wall and clearing it of impurities with picks and other implements, then breaking it into small pieces, had to be done preparatory to lifting it in buckets to the surface by means of winches. Accidents were a constant threat.[64] But the deposits included primary ore material that was said to be the richest ever discovered on earth.[65]

Living conditions in the Upper Peninsula Copper Country in the early years were very rough, with many social problems, including drunkenness. Calumet had numerous bars and a serious alcoholism problem, as also was the case in other mining communities in the area. Infant mortality and childhood illnesses were a threat to families, as was the fear that the breadwinner might be injured or otherwise unable to earn a living. Additional pressure was added as advanced equipment was brought in and more efficiency demanded in the mines. Patience with economic stress during hard times, as well as with the hard work, long hours, and perceived lack of respect, was exhausted for many of the miners in 1913, when the arrival of the radical Western Federation of Miners precipitated a disastrous and violent strike in the region.[66] This culminated in a catastrophe at a hall where a Christmas party for miners' families was in progress upstairs; someone called out "Fire," the door became blocked, and seventy-three died in the panic that resulted. The story is told in a Woody Guthrie ballad: "Take a trip with me in 1913, / To Calumet, in the copper country." The ballad ends with a line, presented as a quote from the parents and miners, directed to the "bosses": "See what your greed for money has done."[67]

The American consul serving at Bergen in 1864, O. E. Dreutzer, seems to have encouraged men to make contractual arrangements that would involve free or low-cost passage on condition of subsequent employment in Upper Peninsula mines. This did not meet with applause from the Norwegian press, to be sure, but in his defense, he disingenuously claimed that his role was only to notarize the contracts made between U.S. immigration companies and those who wished to have a better life. Immigrant workers were offered remission of all transportation costs to Michigan as well as support for housing and food if they would agree to two-year contracts. Pay was to be $260 per annum.[68] One of the immigrant agents was Christian Taftezon, an energetic promoter in 1864–65 for the mines as more desirable places of employment than the farms on the American prairies. His recruits, who were at first from the Tromsø region, were transported to England and sailed from Liverpool or Newcastle. Later he recruited a group, organized to leave for the Copper Country from Trondheim, which would pay a partial fee for their travel and provide their own food. Their entry would be through Quebec.[69]

Norwegians, then, were among those who came to work in the Calumet and Hecla mines, the conglomerate lode that "literally formed the rock upon which Calumet & Hecla [Company] was founded."[70] These mines reached their peak production in 1916, and in fact would remain active for a century, until production ceased in 1969.[71] The town of Calumet was a mining boom-town, its ethnic groups served by numerous churches, each being central to the life of a unit made up of a single nationality within the larger community. The forming of a Norwegian congregation in 1871 thus represented a typical pattern in the town, with a building for worship being constructed on Pine Street the next year. Establishing a church was a priority here as elsewhere among Norwegian immigrants. Norwegians had initially come to Calumet from Alten in the north of Norway six years before, and were sufficient in numbers to call their first pastor, the Rev. Hans Christian Rornas, who had been ordained in the Church of Norway. Other Scandinavians attended at first, but by the end of the decade, they had left to establish their own ethnic churches. The parish church was the center of social activity for Norwegian Americans, as had been the case in their native country, and at Calumet, as in many other churches elsewhere, the Norwegian language was retained in services until the 1920s.

The first church building served until 1899, after property for the con-struction of a new structure had been obtained two years previously from the Calumet and Hecla Mining Company. The driving force behind the proj-ect, and a principal patron, was Edward Ulseth, who had come to Calumet from Kristiansund, where he had been a fisherman and also a boat builder. He arrived in 1881 as a laborer and rose to become one of the town's most prominent citizens. According to his obituary in the *Daily Mining Gazette*, his "interests expanded until they extended to all parts of the copper country and to other sections of the Upper Peninsula, . . . his activities at various times including contracting, building, retail coal, wood and lumber dealing, and real estate development."[72] His home, a stately Victorian mansion, still stands at 416 Eighth Street.

The new church, which despite the loss of its steeple is still standing, is much in need of restoration and is being renovated by the local Norwegian Lutheran Church Historical Society. It is anticipated that when completed, the building will be a museum and meeting place for the local Sons of Norway lodge members interested in their heritage. The church, with an

The Norwegian Lutheran Church at Seventh and Elm Streets in Calumet under con-
struction in 1898. Standing on top of the scaffolding above the steeple is Nils Ulseth (he
is marked with a penciled X in the photograph). Courtesy of the Norwegian Lutheran
Church Historical Society, Calumet.

attached parsonage, is said to have been exactly modeled on the church in
Kristiansund. In many ways, however, it is typical of Norwegian Lutheran
churches constructed in America in the late nineteenth and early twentieth
centuries. It is carpenter Gothic, with stained-glass windows, now severely
damaged, that contain geometric and floral designs. In the chancel, there is
a reredos within a carved frame that is typically Norwegian. The oil painting,

on canvas, shows Jesus walking on the water, reaching out to Peter, who is attempting to do the same feat; the biblical account in Matthew 14:31 has Jesus say to him, "O thou of little faith, wherefore didst thou doubt?" Jesus is dressed ethereally in white. The altar is encircled by an altar rail of typical Norwegian design.

Other features are worth noting. Hymns were accompanied by a Packard reed organ of the type familiar in many other Norwegian Lutheran churches. Over the chancel arch, there remains a pair of wall paintings, at the time of this writing endangered by the condition of the roof. At the right, an angel appears, wearing an alb and holding a scroll with the text "Jesus, er veien, sandheden og livet" ("Jesus is the way, truth, and life," John 14:6); this reaches across the arch to the other side, where an open Bible is displayed. The painting is a very good example of Norwegian folk art. The church had a full basement for Sunday School and confirmation classes as well as social gatherings.

Following World War II, when the copper mines in the area were becoming depleted, the decline of the population of the Calumet area accelerated. The population of 50,000 in 1910 had been reduced to 7,000 in the 2000 census. As in so many other regions that had strong ethnic ties, the next generation would become widely dispersed. Children married and moved away, whether to college or university, or in search of better jobs. By the 1950s, the church was being used only sporadically for services and weddings, and by the late 1980s, the church was more or less derelict. At this time, the village council wanted to have the church and parish house demolished. Fortunately here, as in many other locations, an awareness of the importance of history and heritage would ultimately prevail, though the ultimate fate of the building, which was central for the Norwegian community in the late nineteenth and early twentieth centuries, depends on the determination of those in the town and region who are supporting its renovation.

Another group of Norwegian immigrants arrived between 1870 and 1890 to work in the iron mines in Marquette County, also in the Upper Peninsula. Within only a few years, Ishpeming, on the northern side of the Marquette Iron Range, had acquired several hundred Norwegian immigrants, mainly from the north of Norway, and a Norwegian Lutheran Church had been established there.[73] Smaller communities were initially formed elsewhere, as at Iron Mountain and Ironwood.

Iron mines could be of the open-pit variety, which were much safer for workers, but others were deep-shaft mines that penetrated to iron deposits far below the surface, using technology similar to that which was used in the copper mines. Ports were conveniently located for the Marquette Range and also for the Menominee Range, served by the port at Escanaba. Michigan iron mines were the source of much of the iron used for the rails on which the trains ran that won the West, and their proximity to Detroit, via the Great Lakes, facilitated the use of the metal for America's great car industry in its heyday. Large ore carriers bound for Cleveland were once seen busily passing through Lake St. Claire and down the Detroit River. However, by the early twentieth century, the output of the Michigan iron mines was already being dwarfed by the mines on Minnesota's great Mesabi Range. As with the descendants of Norwegian copper miners, those who grew up on the iron ranges also turned their talents to other occupations, and many have moved away. Later generations appear to have succeeded in living better lives than their parents, so many of whom had been subjected to grinding poverty and daily danger in the workplace.

Ishpeming and Skiing

If logging and mining were the main industries in which Norwegian immigrants participated in the Upper Peninsula, the area is also remembered as a location where skiing as a sport was established in America. In the nineteenth century, Norwegians were familiar with and utilized skiing as a practical way of travel over snow during the long winters—more efficient than the snowshoeing that had been done previously by fur traders and others. Cross-country skiing had been practiced in Norway from prehistoric times, and skis are reported to have been called "ships of the snow" in the Eddas. A "History of Ishpeming Ski Club" begins as follows: "When Odin, one of the greatest gods, went over the mountains to the north of Norway to depose the god Thor, he wore skis. The snows were deep, the grades heavy, and he fashioned a pair of skis to assist in his journey. . . . Certain it is, that the ski has long been in use and that its invention was due to necessity."[74] According to the saga writer Snorre Sturlason, Olaf Trygvason, the Viking king who reigned from 995–1000 C.E., had a reputation as a highly skilled skier. There was even a Norse god of skiing, whose name was Ullr. A famous event in national history occurred in 1206 C.E. when the two-year-old prince Håkon Håkonsson was rescued by two members of the Birkebeiner (Birchleg) party from Lillehammer who carried him away on skis to safety—a journey of fifty kilometers. Before Sweden gained sovereignty over Norway in 1814, ski troops had helped to defend the country against that neighbor, and not surprisingly thereafter, the Swedes worked to dismantle that force.[75]

However, the practice of organizing ski competitions was also a Norwegian import. Just as in the New World the term *ski* was a direct loan word from Norwegian (Old Norse *skith*), so later would the racing term *slalom* be borrowed from the Norwegian *slalaam* when competitive races were established.

The recognition of skiing as a sport is especially associated with Ishpeming.[76] In 1887 the Norden Ski Club, comprised of about fifteen members, was founded there, with a local tournament following in January 1888.[77] Skis of ten-foot length, each with a ski pole of ash that was six feet in length, had been made by cabinetmaker Haagen Asgaard, an outfit that cost between eight and ten dollars each—a substantial amount in those days. There was, however, no standard size or design. A ski slide had been built for the 1888 contest; ski jumping would be featured and prizes offered, with Ole Sundie of Ishpeming receiving the medal that year for jumping 35 feet.

The skis used initially were modeled on those that had been used in Norway—seven to fourteen feet long, with straps into which the skier's boots would be inserted. Children's skis were made thus, usually about six feet in length, up to World War II. Some were decorated, as in the Old Country. In the Upper Peninsula and elsewhere in the Midwest, they were generally made of birch, pine, or ash. One ski pole continued to be used rather than the two that became standard later. In 1900 Aksel Holter was making skis of the Norwegian type at Ishpeming that sold for between fifty cents and seven dollars.

A more vigorous move was made in 1901 with the founding of the Ishpeming Ski Club, which opened membership to "men of all nationalities of good character." Norwegian was dropped in favor of English for meetings. Interest in skiing at this time was clearly high in the area, and 10 percent of the local population was reported by then to be on skis in the winter. The budget for this year's event was $500, and a scoring system was devised. Two contestants jumped more than 77 feet in pursuit of the prize of ten dollars. The reporter for the *Marquette Mining Journal*, writing on February 23, called the jump "desperate in the extreme." Admission was charged for the event, and by February 1904 it was reported that 10,000 spectators came to Ishpeming, where the ski hill was decorated with U.S. and Norwegian colors, both of which are red, white, and blue. The Ishpeming Ski Club, which now

A set of late nineteenth- or early twentieth-century skis. The adjustable leather foot straps are missing, but the location of the slot into which they would have been passed through the ski can be observed by the dark-colored skid plate on the left ski. Photograph: T. L. Wolvert.

advertises itself as the nation's "oldest continuously active ski club," was host to the 2008 Junior Olympics.

Ishpeming was logically the location for the launching in 1905 of the National Ski Association, the organization that was crucial in establishing skiing as a national sport.[78] Yet even here, of the seven founding members, six were Norwegians, and Michigan dominated the governing board. Impetus for the organization had come especially from its president, Carl Tellefsen, who had come to Michigan from Trondheim, along with Aksel Holter, its tireless secretary. In the association's first year, President Theodore Roosevelt was invited to be present as a guest at the first annual competition, but he was not able to attend. The organization's yearbook, *Skisport*, extolled the value of skiing as morally uplifting—a belief that, though imported from Norway, would have appealed to President Roosevelt. Ishpeming would be the location chosen for the National Ski Hall of Fame and Museum.

Competitions and ski jumping gave wide visibility and recognition to skiing as a sport, and skiers from Michigan, Wisconsin, and Minnesota continued to dominate. Longer and longer ski jumps were created, with Ishpeming and Munising competing with Minnesota and Wisconsin sites for a world record. A record of 122 feet at Ishpeming in February 1908 broke the previous record, but a month later, the title had to be surrendered to Duluth.[79] By this year, skiing was being proposed as an Olympic sport, and Nordic dominance would thereafter continue for another two decades. A tradition of skiing is still maintained at Ishpeming, where Suicide Hill still remains the location popular for ski jumping.

Bridges, Tunnels, and Motorcars

Technically trained engineers from Norway were widely welcomed from the time of the American Civil War—a period of welcome that lasted eighty years. During this time, hundreds of engineers came to this country in order to work. Young graduates saw America as the land of opportunity, and indeed for them it was just that. The fact that the young members of this profession who came to the United States had looser ties to cultural and religious traditions of the homeland seems also have been a factor in their willingness to emigrate.[80] Robert Bjork, in his book *Saga in Steel and Concrete: Norwegian Engineers in America,* quotes an immigrant who worked in the Midwest concerning his reasons, first of all economic, for leaving Norway. This man knew that "he would not feel as much at home in a foreign country as in Norway, but that did not deter him. . . . He was young, unmarried, and wanted to see a little of the world, especially the 'big proposition' country which he had heard so much about."[81] In 1880 the civil engineer Alfred W. Gjerdrun, who had come to work on the Flint and Pere Marquette Railroad, wrote to the *Skandinaven,* the Norwegian-language newspaper published in Chicago, that he had been "well received."[82] Some of the most distinguished to come to Michigan would build bridges and tunnels and achieve recognition in the motor car industry centered in Detroit.

Ingolf Erdal, who had studied at Trondheim, was associated with a Chicago firm as chief engineer when, in 1938, he designed and built a bridge over the Saginaw River at Bay City that was given a prestigious award for incorporating the most advanced design for an elevated expressway. In this bridge, which had three spans, allowance was made to permit river traffic.[83] Knud Sophus Riser, from Christiania, had previously worked in Detroit and other locations before he assumed the leadership of the Grand Rapids Bridge Company in 1901. The *Transactions* of the American Society of Civil Engineers for 1932 cited Riser as being the final authority in every aspect of design involving steel in bridges.[84] L. E. Sangdahl, also trained in Christiania, was responsible for the layout of the bridge that provided a connection between the city and Belle Isle in the Detroit River.[85]

A much more spectacular achievement, however, was the Michigan Central rail tunnel between Detroit and Windsor that was built in 1906–10. Spurring this achievement was the opening of a railroad tunnel between Michigan and Canada at Port Huron in 1891, a route that would have been disadvantageous to Detroit businesses. Following preliminary design work, the Norwegian engineer Olaf Hoff produced a novel conception that refined the previous plans and thus made an underwater tunnel possible in this location. The tunnel was to be set into a trench that had been dredged in the river, into which parallel giant steel tubes would be lowered. These were encased in concrete, and after water was removed, another layer was introduced inside them. The entire process, including the pumping of water from the sections of tunnel and the installation of the ventilation system, was considered ingenious.[86]

A better-known tunnel, however, is the busy Detroit-Windsor automobile tunnel—5,137 feet in length—which was opened to traffic in 1930 after being under construction for two-and-one-half years. This project benefited from Hoff's pioneer work as well as that of another Norwegian engineer, Ole Singstad, the latter also responsible for the design of the Holland Tunnel at New York. The actual engineer of the Detroit-Windsor tunnel was Soren A. Thoresen, likewise from Norway.[87] Seven hundred thousand tons of clay had to be removed by men—sometimes called "sandhogs"—who were protected by a shield that was thirty-two feet in height. Progress was no more than ten feet per day. The resulting trench in the river was 2,454 feet in length. Into this, the nine sections of heavy structural steel tubes, 250

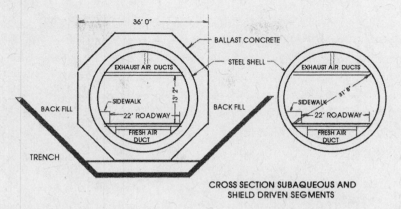

CROSS SECTION SUBAQUEOUS AND
SHIELD DRIVEN SEGMENTS

Scale drawing of Detroit-Windsor Tunnel. Dennis Darling, after engineers' construction plan.

feet in length, were moved into place by barges, then lowered, and finally connected together.[88]

With the expectation of heavy motorcar traffic, huge ventilation fans were required. The work took from the summer of 1928 until November 1930, when the first vehicles were able to pass through the tunnel.[89] It was the greatest achievement in underwater tunneling up to that time and considered an engineering marvel. The tunnel remains a major link between the United States and Canada.

At the time when the Detroit-Windsor tunnel was completed, the automobile had come into its own as a means of transportation, in large part because of the innovations effected by Henry Ford and the Ford Motorcar Company. Numerous Norwegians and Norwegian Americans came to the Detroit area during these years of development of the industry to work on the assembly lines. Others were important figures in management and in the development of new manufacturing techniques. One was Trygve Jolstad, assistant manager of the Briggs Manufacturing Company in Detroit. Jolstad played an important role in the development of improved automobile bodies during the 1920s, prior to his death at the end of the decade. Another who seems to have been important in many respects, from engine design to automobile suspension systems, was N. H. N. Olsen, whom Bjork describes as "another colorful Detroit engineer."[90] Olsen was an originator of the experimental division in 1930 at Ford, where he had begun working in 1915 in the production

Harry B. Hanson, Engineer

Hanson's father was from Sogn, the county in Norway from which his mother's parents had also emigrated. With a degree from Iowa State University at Ames, he joined the Ford Motor Company and rose to become one of the most important of Henry Ford's engineers, serving as head of engineering activities from 1929. Highly competent, he was the chief of planning for the massive River Rouge factory, which presented huge problems to be solved. "The River Rouge site couldn't have been worse," he said, since the stable bedrock on which it was set was a hundred feet below the surface.* Hanson also had a hand in designing and constructing the

Harry B. Hanson (1884–1949) was prominent in the Ford Motor Company. Courtesy of the Norwegian-American Historical Association Archives at St. Olaf College.

Henry Ford Museum. He is perhaps best known as the designer of the Willow Run airport and bomber factory in 1941–42. In the planning stage, the location was, he noted, an ideal spot for the purpose: "Out there in those wide open spaces," he said, "we had plenty of elbow room."† The architect chosen for realizing the plan was the famous Albert Kahn. In the end the complex, costing $47,620,000, sprawled over eighty acres, held seven runways, and was the home of one of the largest factories in the world, where up to 42,000 employees worked. More than 8,500 B-24 "Liberator" bombers rolled off the assembly line. The airport remains a very active hub, though passenger service was transferred to Detroit Metro Airport by the 1960s.‡

* Allan Nevins and Frank Ernest Hill, *Ford: Decline and Rebirth* (New York: Charles Scribner's Sons, 1963), 290–91.
† Ibid., 187.
‡ See *Detroit News*, May 23, 1963; clipping in Norwegian-American Historical Association Archives, Northfield, MN, p. 877.

department. During World War II, he was in charge of the Hexagon Tool and Engineering Corporation of Dearborn, Michigan; this corporation produced "artillery items" at that time.[91] A photo in the Norwegian-American Historical Association archives shows him receiving an Army-Navy Production Award in July 1944 from Major Nelson W. McCormick for his defense work.[92]

Rolf (Ralph) Helgeby as a young pilot in the Norwegian Air Force. The airplane is one that he flew when in the service of his native country. Photo courtesy of the Bentley Historical Library, University of Michigan.

As the technological edge in the motorcar industry shifted to General Motors, a significant contribution was provided by E. K. Wemmerlund. At the time he was first employed, in 1911, General Motors was just then emerging from bankruptcy. He became director of production engineering for the company, and by applying the new techniques of "scientific management" developed by Frederick Winslow Taylor with the assistance of the Norwegian Carl G. Barth, he became "a leading developer of incentive wage plans, especially by machine tenders and assembly line workers."[93] It is said that Wemmerlund was able to achieve the objective of making "production flow like a river."[94]

While Barth, a remarkable mathematician and a descendant of King Harald Fairhair of Norway, was not actually a Michigan resident, his contribution to the state's industry merits recognition. His contribution made possible precision work with alloy steel. His slide rules reduced the guesswork of previous metal cutting to scientific exactness, and his belief that pay ought to be commensurate with the amount and quality of work produced a revolution in factory management.[95]

As a pioneer airman who began flying in 1916, Rolf O. Helgeby (1897–82) was chosen for the Royal Norwegian Air Force during World War I, even surviving a plane crash in a Farman Shorthorn biplane when running low on fuel while flying across a valley shrouded in fog. On August 17, 1919, he was the second pilot to land at Trondheim, the first having landed earlier the same day, and the first to fly from there to Oslo—a flight of 350 miles over the mountains.[96]

Helgeby was from a distinguished family: his father was a professor and for a time superintendent of the Agricultural College of Norway, and his brother became ambassador to the Soviet Union. After his move to Flint, Michigan, in 1925, he became an American citizen and anglicized his name to Ralph. His employment was with the A/C Spark Plug Division, where he was an experimental engineer and responsible for numerous patents for General Motors. In 1930 he came into possession of an open-cockpit Model One Fleet Trainer, made by the Consolidated Aircraft Corporation, and after the Nazi invasion of Norway flew to Canada to help train Norwegian pilots at the camp established for the purpose at Muskoka, Canada. He also played a role in the Norwegian Relief effort to bring aid to those in his home country who were suffering from oppression—and later, after the war, its effects. His papers, in the Bentley Historical Library at the University of Michigan, contain many photographs and clippings about his career as an airman, and also indicate his sympathy for the plight of Norway during the occupation. The Greater Flint affiliate of the Experimental Aircraft Association is named the Ralph O. Helgeby Chapter in his memory.

Diversity of Gifts

Norwegians and their descendants brought an energy to America that they funneled into a variety of occupations. If first-generation Norwegians worked deep underground in the mines, the next would move up to positions with the same company that would keep them on the surface, or they would go into entirely different lines of work. The same would tend to be true of those who sailed the Great Lakes. Susan Rokicki, a music teacher at Calumet, reported that her grandfather, Peder Tobiassen Faksvåg, had come to America in 1899 from Solligård, near Kleive, to work as a carpenter in the mines. Most of her cousins are engineers, while her brother is a businessman and her sister is a speechwriter for the Federal Deposit Insurance Corporation (FDIC). Wayne Roy Stordahl, a professional engineer and CEO of U.P. Engineering and Architectural Associates before his retirement, is a descendant of Peter Ludvig Stordahl, who left Christiania in 1882 and settled in Muskegon because it was a port city; from there he would sail as a ship captain.[97]

Some, like the engineers noted above, came to Michigan already having trained in the Old Country. Others, like the builder Edward Ulseth of Calumet, simply seemed to have a knack for entrepreneurship. Frederick Braastad, who came to Michigan in 1865, would establish a successful department store in Ishpeming and would serve as mayor of that town. He was also one of the founders of the National Ski Association in 1905. But perhaps more significantly, he was the first Norwegian to be elected to state office in Lansing, when he was selected as state treasurer for a two-year term in 1890. Also, he likely stood above his countrymen in his artistic tastes, since he would send his daughter Borghild to Northwestern University to study music, whereupon she ventured forth on a serious career as a vocal solo-ist.[98] In 1981 his descendants in turn established in his memory the Braastad Nature Sanctuary, northwest of Ishpeming, which was dedicated by his son, Frederick W. Braastad, M.D., and other members of his family in 1981.

Of course, the majority had come from Norway with humble skills and goals, which might differ from farming, sailing, or mining. Among these, however, many still retained their connection with the soil. For example, Nils Andreas Olsen, a member of a branch of the Bjorn family in Norway, was a shipbuilder at Whitehall and then worked as a carpenter in the construction of houses, churches, and spinning wheels, but did not abandon farming.[99] On the whole, those who had mastered the English language appear to have seen their choice of occupation range from the line of work of their fathers to seemingly endless possibilities. Norwegian American schoolboys might even be encouraged by their teachers to dream of being President someday.

Nevertheless, persons with little formal education could manage surpris-ingly well when they had the energy and intelligence to do so. Arthur W. Thurner takes note of members of the Frimodig family, who came in 1871 to work in the Quincy Mine with the hope of a better life than offered in Norway at Kaafjord copper mines. One member of the family stands out, as Thurner explains:

> Isaac Frimodig, who had begun work at age eleven in Norway attended school briefly, then worked at the Quincy, Calumet and Hecla, Centennial, and Osceola Mines before entering the mercantile business at Red Jacket. By 1894, he was elected by Republicans to serve as Houghton County trea-surer. A member of several lodges, . . . he also championed prohibition. He returned to Norway when he was twenty-one, worked for two years, married, and came back to the Copper Country.[100]

Occupations that naturally seemed to open up for Norwegian Ameri-cans might range from forestry and industry to journalism and academia, among many others. The large areas of forest, and those areas that had been

David Frimodig, Forester and Local Historian

The Norwegian American David Frimodig (1922–95) was usually known by his nickname, "Mac." Born at Houghton, he attended Michigan Technical University following military service in World War II, during which he served in the Tenth Mountain Division ski troops. As a forester, he became regional director for all the state parks in the Upper Peninsula in 1963 until his retirement. He was recognized for organizing interpretive centers at state parks and historical displays at the Marquette County Historical Museum and the National Ski Hall of Fame in Ishpeming. His service to the Marquette County Historical Society included the office of president as well as contributor to its quarterly journal. He also was a member of several other local historical and natural-history associations, including the Houghton County Historical Association and the Keweenaw Historical Association.*

Frimodig's work as a local historian also resulted in three publications for the Fort Wilkins Natural History Association that were issued with the cooperation of the Michigan Department of Natural Resources. These were *The Fort Wilkins Story* (1980), *The Copper Harbor Stare* (1969), and *Shipwrecks off Keweenaw* (c.1974). In 1990 his *Keweenaw Character: The Foundation of Michigan Copper Country* was issued. Additionally he served as publisher of coloring books, two of which were *Northern Michigan's Wildlife and Wild Flowers* and *Copper Country Coloring Book*.

* Information from the Marquette County Historical Society.

clear-cut in the western Lower Peninsula as well as in the Upper Peninsula presented a need for foresters to attend to them. Pete Peterson, who had been brought to Michigan from Kristiansund at six years of age, worked in the automobile business—first with Buick after completing high school, and then for Studebaker until a troubled merger in 1954, after which he did not return to the state but went on to become president of the company that built Mack trucks. In such cases as this, Michigan was the training ground for Norwegian American expertise that benefited management in American industry outside the state.[101]

The Frankfort newspaper, the *Record Patriot*, owned and edited by Norwegian Americans, was passed on to Peter Sandman, and then to his son Jeff

Sandman, who is giving focus to events in local history. An example would be his story about the visit to Benzonia in 1917 by the young Ernest Hemingway and his family, who were traveling north to the Petoskey area.[102] A relative, John E. Peterson, also was in this line of work and had a substantial journalism career over twenty-five years with the *Detroit News*. Peterson was the winner of awards for his reporting, and the head of his newspaper's Washington Bureau. He reported, under his byline, on topics that ranged from automobile safety to the Vietnam and Gulf wars. One story on February 3, 1971, predicted angry public demonstrations if Laos were to be attacked—demonstrations that would in fact occur and that led to the Kent State University affair when four students were killed and nine wounded.

The contributions of Norwegian Americans to academia in Michigan have been even more extensive. While Scandinavian studies departments do not exist in the state's universities as such, specialists in other fields have been numerous and sometimes unusual, as in the case of David Ede (1935–2008), a seminary graduate and the son of a Norwegian pastor, who became a recognized authority on Islam and chairman of the comparative religion department at Western Michigan University. Margery Stomne Selden, a retired musicologist at one time on the faculty of Wayne State University, has recently had some success as a hymn writer, even having her work published in China—with the words presented in Chinese translation, of course.

At Michigan State University, Lawrence M. Sommers (1919–2007), the son of Norwegian immigrants and the first of his family to graduate from college, was a faculty member in the geography department from 1949 to 1989 and during that time served as head of his department for twenty-four years. A driving force for creating a national reputation for his department, he was instrumental in the development of the International Studies Center and international programs. He had obtained his Ph.D. from Northwestern University, where he took up the study of commercial fishing in Norway. This was the beginning of an interest in Scandinavian economic geography that he sustained throughout his career. Ultimately he would be the author of more than a hundred publications in the field of economic and applied geography, and was influential in Scandinavian geographic organizations and others in the field. He was a founding member of the Applied Geography Conference. In connection with his work, he traveled to Norway more than thirty times, and also to other locations on five continents.[103] Michigan

State University's bicentennial project in 1976 was the *Atlas of Michigan*, which he edited. This impressive volume had as its purpose the presentation of the "varied physical and cultural characteristics" of Michigan, with even an eye to the way the Ice Age determined the "natural landscape." Other aspects ranged from average temperatures over the years in various parts of the state to religious preferences as these differed from county to county.[104]

Two Norwegian professors at Andrews University rate the designation "distinguished." The late Hans-Jørgen Holman (1925–86) was born in Drammen and was living in Norway during the German occupation, at which time he participated in the Resistance. After early study in the sciences, he became an active musicologist and practicing musician, sometimes performing in or directing twenty or more concerts in a single year. Related to this, he was a prolific editor of early music for his performances, especially for the Andrews Capella da Camera, which he directed. His particular expertise was in Norwegian music of the Middle Ages and paleography, and he used this knowledge also in connection with his ethnomusicological study of the religious folk tunes of Norway. His knowledge was encyclopedic, but sadly very little of it was published in his lifetime. Instead, much work was disseminated at conferences both in Michigan at such venues as the International Congress on Medieval Studies at Kalamazoo, and abroad at conferences like the meeting of the International Musicological Society or the International Folk Music Council.

Another Norwegian at the same institution, Øystein S. LaBianca, was also born in Norway and remains a Norwegian national. As a sociocultural anthropologist and archaeologist, Professor LaBianca has been involved with archaeological digs at Tall Hisban in Jordan, where he has applied an entirely new methodology for studying food systems and ways of knowing about how people moved back and forth between a sedentary and a nomadic life as conditions changed between the late Bronze Age and modern times. One of the mechanisms involved should be of particular interest today: the management of the local water level. Significantly, he finds that settlement intensity was in direct relation to larger historical and political developments such as the rise of the Byzantine or Mamluk empire. Professor LaBianca is currently vice president of the American Schools of Oriental Research, and visiting researcher at the University of Bergen, Norway.

Rudolph Gjelsness, distinguished librarian at the University of Michigan. Photo: University of Michigan Archives, courtesy of the Bentley Historical Library.

Among the many Norwegian American academics in Michigan universities, Rudolph H. Gjelsness (1894–1968) also stands out.[105] He was professor and chairman of the University of Michigan's Department of Library Science from 1940 to 1965, and was one of the most influential librarians of his time. He first came to the University of Michigan in 1925 after a year-long fellowship in Norway funded by the American Scandinavian Foundation, and stayed until 1932, when he moved to the New York Public Library and Columbia University. By 1937 he was back at the University of Michigan, where he would remain until his retirement. His activities during this period were not confined to Michigan, however, for he was active in a summer school at Bogotá in 1942 and spent 1943–44 on leave in Mexico City, where he taught at the National School of Anthropology. He was a consultant for the university library at Baghdad in 1962–63. His work for the American Library Association was extensive and impressive, and for a time he served as president of the Association of American Library Schools. Among his publications, which included many specialist articles and books, was a translation of *Lisbeth of Jarnfjeld* by the Norwegian writer Johan Falkberget. For his

A Norwegian Nurse

In spite of the generally healthy Norwegian American population in the late nineteenth and early twentieth centuries, illness when it did occur could be serious. Measles and scarlet fever were threats to children in those days, and tuberculosis was a potential scourge for all. Remedies learned in Norway could be effective, sometimes more so than what was then regarded as "modern" medicine. However, when a bone needed to be set or special care was required for a pneumonia patient, there were at first only a few facilities outside larger urban centers. The situation was particularly critical for those living in the Upper Peninsula, where for some, the closest fully equipped hospital might be at Duluth. Cottage hospitals, like those established in the 1890s in Marquette—a system that eventually evolved into Marquette General Hospital—had to fill the gap.[*] As train transportation and, later, ambulance service became available, patients from outlying regions in the Lower Peninsula could be transported to hospitals in the region or even to Detroit, or to the University Hospital in Ann Arbor.

One of the first students admitted to the new nursing program at the University of Michigan was Ellen Baver, who has been mentioned in connection with her family's immigration from Norway when she was sixteen, and subsequently her service as a maid for a local family. It was when she accompanied her sister Mary (Marit), who had polio (then called infantile paralysis), to the University Hospital in 1890 that Ellen learned about plans there for instituting instruction in nursing. She was one of the six students who enrolled in the program in 1891. After her graduation in 1894, she returned to her home town in the northwest Lower Peninsula to work as a nurse, and three years later married Dr. Frank LaRue, who received his medical training at Rochester, New York; at Bellevue Hospital in New York City; and at the University of Virginia. He had served as a physician with the U.S. Marine Corps, and graduated from the Grand Rapids College of Medicine.

Together, Ellen and her husband set up a medical practice in their house in Elberta in 1906 and continued until Dr. LaRue died in 1949,[†] only two years before a modern hospital to serve the region was completed in nearby Frankfort. They worked together as a team to deliver babies, perform surgery, and care for the injured. The infirmary and the doctor's office were on the first floor, the latter outfitted with professional books, examination chair or table, and required equipment to perform medical examinations. For the patients' rooms, one went up a winding staircase to the second floor. Ellen had responsibility for the care of the inpatients, including their meals and their linens.

The facilities and surgical techniques used by the LaRues will seem primitive today, but since they lived in a time when the danger of bacteria was well understood, their attention to cleanliness and sterilization of surgical equipment perhaps made their cottage hospital safer than many modern hospitals, which have become notorious for staphylococcus infections. Long hospital stays were needed after surgery, and much greater care had to be taken than today to maintain a sterile environment. Surgical equipment was subjected to sterilization by boiling or heating in an oven. Nurses, who generally functioned more like nurse practitioners, administered ether, or later a safer and more effective form of anesthesia. Sodium Pentothal was not available until after World War II, too late for Ellen and her husband.[‡]

Doctors regularly made house calls. Even in small communities and after the arrival of the motorcar, these were not always without difficulty. In the area where heavy lake-effect snow was prevalent and when snowplowing was as yet not done with any regularity, driving was often frustrating and hazardous. Ellen on many occasions accompanied "Dr. Frank" on such missions of mercy, especially when a birth was expected. An account by Ena Jackson gives the story of one such house call when the couple's car became stuck on the middle of a steep, snow-covered hill south of Elberta. Ellen's husband asked her to step out of the car to help push. When the car began to move, he kept on driving up the hill. She followed, walking, but at the top she saw no car. Fortunately, there was a farmhouse at hand where she could find refuge from the cold. Dr. LaRue had completely forgotten her, and was only reminded when he came to the waiting family "and was met with the question, 'Where is Ellen?' (rather anxiously, I might add)," to which he "turned to look behind him and said, 'Well, I guess I must have left her in the middle of Stratton Hill.'" It was not a moment of amusement, since, as Jackson explains, "Ellen's expertise was very helpful, and the families looked forward to having her on the job."[§]

At the end of the cottage hospital era, the last one in Frankfort was about to shutter its doors in May of 1944. Another Norwegian American, Arthur Peterson, was asked to include a notice of impending closure in the *Benzie County Patriot*, which he edited and published along with his wife Helen. However, he instead successfully raised the necessary funds to keep the little hospital open until the new Paul Oliver Hospital was ready to receive patients.**

* St. Luke's/Marquette General Hospital Collection, MS. 90; abstract, http:// library.nmu.edu/archives/collections/selected/mgh.htm, accessed December 6, 2008. For early hospitals in the Keweenaw Peninsula, see Thurner, *Strangers and Sojourners*, 167–68, 337 n. 25.
† Kay Hommel et al., *Shared Moments: A Journey through Time* (Benzonia, MI: Benzie Area Historical Society, 2007), 173 (photograph). The house has been restored.
‡ For information about treatment in cottage hospitals in the Frankfort area, see Ena Kraft Jackson, *A Nurse Remembers: Generations of Loving Care, Birth, Bandages and Bedpans* (Frankfort, MI: Frankfort-Elberta Schools Foundation, 2001).
§ Ibid., 5.
** Ibid., 22–23.

accomplishments, Professor Gjelsness was awarded honorary doctorates from Luther College and the University of North Dakota. He was always formal, expecting to be addressed as "Mr. Gjelsness" even by colleagues. Yet he was described as "unpretentious" and as a "learned and gentle man," qualities that were always valued by Norwegian Americans. He was noted for his patience with his students, and it was said that he "taught as much or more outside the classroom as in it." During his tenure as department chairman, 2,269 degrees, including 47 doctorates, were awarded in library science at the University of Michigan. When he retired, he was presented with a *Festschrift*, a volume of essays in his honor entitled *Books in America's Past*, edited by David Kaser and published by the University Press of Virginia.

The Religion of Norwegian Americans

The first Norwegian church to be built in Michigan was the First Evangelical Lutheran Church in Muskegon. Previously, Norwegians there had been members of a generic Scandinavian Lutheran congregation, then started meeting together at Olson Hall in 1864, and finally built their own church at Hall and Prospect Streets in 1867. Their first resident pastor, the Rev. Hans J. Bergh, arrived two years later.[106] This structure no longer is extant, but a typical church interior may be seen in Bethany Evangelical Lutheran Church at Northport. The Norwegian Lutheran Church founded in 1871 in Calumet, in the Upper Peninsula, has already been mentioned. These are but three of many Norwegian churches established in the late nineteenth century and the early part of the twentieth century. They were none of them officially organized under the control of the hierarchy of the Church of Norway, which was part of the state bureaucracy without a missionary mandate. Of course, the Church of Norway was the mother church for all the American churches of this denomination serving this ethnic group.

The establishment of the Norwegian Church as a state institution dates from the Reformation of the sixteenth century. This state church, ostensibly Lutheran, at first functioned under the Danish Crown. Until 1811, the date of the founding of Norway's first university, the clergy were trained in Denmark and essentially were part of the Dano-Norwegian elite. However,

The interior of Bethel Evangelical Lutheran Church at Northport. The church lacks a chancel arch and has the altar set off from the nave only by a typical altar rail. The sanctuary lamp is not here indicative of reserved sacrament; like the Paschal candle and the banner, it is a "modern" addition to the fabric. Photo: Dennis Darling.

throughout the nineteenth century, Danes and Dano-Norwegians continued to dominate the clerical ranks. While the parish provided the center of local community life, there was very often a division between the common folk and the priests, who served as pastors and were officially in charge of their parishioners' religious lives.[107] The folk often felt that the clergy spoke a different language, since many local dialects, especially in the north and west of Norway, differed significantly from Danish and Dano-Norwegian.

Especially outside the major towns, the folk pursued their own ways in matters of spirituality, and in outlying regions of the country, they applied their own distinct musical traditions of musical tuning, intonation, and the use of melisma when singing the Lutheran hymns in church—much to the distress of the authorities, who thought they were simply ignorant country people.[108] These critics had no sympathy for oral tradition. Except in the cities, the hymns were led not by a trained musician but by a *klokker*, who would put his own stamp on the music.[109] Religious songs were also commonly sung in homes, where freedom from constraints of church practice also in turn affected local musical practice. If instruments were allowed to perform along with vocal music, these too would be an influence on Norwegian traditions, but there were limitations on this practice in churches.[110] The best known instrument, the Hardanger fiddle, was regarded as secular and even the devil's instrument[111] and was not allowed inside the church. However, current research into performance practice related to it throws light on the distinctiveness to be found in earlier Norwegian folk music, some of it retained as people emigrated in the nineteenth century. The potential for differences between clergy and the people also did not die out with the transplantation of the church to America.[112]

In Norway as in Denmark, the introduction of Pietism, with its emphasis on personal religion and puritanical ethics, was the force behind a more definitive break with the traditional religion and its expression, in part inherited from the Middle Ages. In 1796 the indefatigable lay preacher Hans Nielsen Hauge came upon the scene and inspired a national revival akin to the Great Awakening in America. In spite of persecution, even time in jail, he did not leave the national church. His influence on some of those who emigrated was profound in that in the New World, Norwegian Lutherans broke up into several church branches competing for membership.[113] At Muskegon, for example, Our Savior's Lutheran Church was formed subsequent to the First Evangelical Lutheran Church as a Haugean congregation.

Hauge's ideas also filtered down further to influence those, a minority to be sure, who then found themselves more comfortable joining with other American denominations such as the Methodists and Baptists. Some who came to the southwest corner of Michigan were drawn to Adventism, which holds a unique place in the spectrum of American religion not only on account of its piety and unique theology but also because of its emphasis on health, nutrition, and healing.[114] Norwegian American missionaries arrived from an Adventist settlement in Wisconsin, and there was further immigration to this area directly from Norway. A Norwegian presence has long been present at Andrews University in Berrien Springs, an institution that had its origins in Battle Creek College, moving to its new site in 1901.

At the opposite end of the spectrum were the options of becoming Episcopalian, Roman Catholic, or secular, sometimes freethinking. Most, of course, remained Lutheran in one form or another, with both an overemphasis on Luther's dictum of "faith alone," and the Pietists' emphasis on personal religious experience placing their mark one way or another on the spirituality of many Norwegian Americans. The Norwegian American sense of personal guilt is well known. By 1917 Norwegian Lutheranism had begun the long process of coming together that culminated eventually in the formation of what is now the largest current Lutheran body, the Evangelical Lutheran Church of America (ELCA), which has a loose form of episcopal governance. There are now close relations between ELCA and the American Episcopal Church, which, to be sure, now has numerous Norwegian Americans as members of its congregations.

From the standpoint of ecclesiastical organization, Hauge's influence was most direct on those synods that may be termed "low church," maintaining a scaled-back liturgy and insisting on the power of the laity in governance. The last half of the nineteenth century was marred by constant disputes over orthodoxy and practice that occurred among the clergy of the mainline Norwegian Lutheran Synod and the others.[115] One of the sources of trouble lay in the relationship with another Lutheran body, the German Missouri Synod, which had influenced some of the Norwegian pastors in the matter of doctrine, particularly into accepting articles of faith not felt to be consistent with the Church of Norway or with the preferences of most Norwegian

Americans. The Missouri Synod had adopted the Formula of Concord of 1577 that affirmed original sin and the inerrancy of the Bible, and denied free will and the role of merit in justification before God.[116] There were even clergy who argued that slavery, abolished as a result of the American Civil War, was not contradicted by the Bible—an idea that was anathema to the Norwegian American laity. Unlike the orthodoxy espoused by many in the Missouri Synod in the nineteenth century, Norwegian Lutherans never accepted the idea that they might possess the only "pure" form of Christianity.

If some of the theological arguments seemed rather distant to Michigan Lutherans, their devotion, or lack of it, to the retention of the Norwegian language was another matter. More isolated communities were likely to maintain Norwegian services longer than urban areas such as Detroit. The change was not without considerable conflict. There is a story, surely apocryphal, about the little old lady speaking up in a meeting and saying, "If Norwegian was good enough for the apostle Paul, it is good enough for me." For clergy with poor English too, the transition could be difficult. In one instance, at an unspecified location, a pastor could not recall the way to ask the members of the congregation to continue to stand until the service had ended, and said, "And the audience will be standing till we all pass away."[117] But change did come, and accelerated after World War I. The majority of congregations in the United States then still used Norwegian, but this quickly eroded until, by the 1930s, Norwegian on a regular basis was a rarity.[118]

Many among the second- and third-generation descendants of the original immigrants wished to achieve amalgamation into the American scene. This movement was in part driven by the encounter with anti-immigrant prejudice. But some strongly felt that it was important to maintain ties with the motherland and its traditions. One of these was the novelist O. E. Rølvaag, who was particularly concerned that ties be maintained through the church. His *Boat of Longing* in particular dwells on the alienation and potential tragedy of life lived by an immigrant in an America without religious and cultural roots. Pastor Kaldahl in his novel *Their Father's God* says, *"A people that has lost its traditions is doomed!"* [119]

Several hymn collections with Norwegian texts had been published in the nineteenth century, and immigrants more often than not came with one of the available Norwegian hymnals tucked away in their luggage. These had texts only. The perceived need for an English-language Lutheran hymnal with musical notation was, however, acknowledged, and cooperation (always problematic among the contentious branches of Norwegian Lutheranism) was attained for preparing one that could be universally adopted. An English-language hymnal was thereafter adopted by the United Norwegian Lutheran Church, the Norwegian Evangelical Lutheran Synod, and Hauge's Evangelical Lutheran Synod in 1913.[120] Some debt to other American churches was acknowledged. The liturgical texts in the *Lutheran Hymnary* (1913) were adapted from the translations used by the American Episcopal Church, with biblical texts taken from the Authorized Version of 1611, and its hymnody likewise was not purely Norwegian. For example, the first hymn in the collection is a psalm tune by Louis Bourgeois applied to a fourth-century text in translation, and there is a very large selection from the English Protestant repertoire—though it does come as a surprise to see sentimental songs such as "Just as I am, without one plea." One of the members of those responsible for selection was F. Melius Christiansen, the founder of a choral tradition at St. Olaf College in Minnesota that has had an important influence on musical practice in Michigan as well. Unsurprisingly, there was a conscious effort to incorporate the "rich treasury of hymns and chorales from the Mother Church," which, it was hoped, could thus be transmitted to "her children" and to be generally attractive to other "English bodies of the Church of the Reformation." The seventy-two Norwegian and Danish or Dano-Norwegian hymns in English translation include many by such hymn writers as Bishop Thomas Kingo, N. F. S. Gruntvig, and H. A. Brorson,[121] and there are German chorale settings by, for example, Johann Crüger, Hans Leo Hassler, Johann Walther, Melchior Franck, and Johann Hermann Schein. Several Norwegian and Dano-Norwegian hymns were particularly loved—for example, Brorson's "Behold a host, arrayed in white" ("Den store hvite flokk"), appearing both with the melody by Ludvig Lindeman and in the folk-tune version that is still retained in the *Norsk Salme Bok* used today in the Church of Norway.[122]

All the hymns were arranged according to the church year, with separate sections for confirmation, marriages, burials, etc. Efforts were made to connect with Norwegian traditions of church worship while at the same time incorporating a great many less-familiar English tunes and, especially, texts. Yet in some ways, the hymnal may be regarded as superior to later collections and speaks well for the work of the editorial committee, which was made up of representatives of both the "high church" and "low church"

Be-hold a host, ar-rayed in white, Like thousand snow-clad mountains bright,
Lo, these are they, of glo-rious fame, Who from the great af-fliction came,

With palms they stand—Who are this band Be - fore the throne of light?
And in the flood of Je - sus' blood Are cleansed from guilt and blame;

Now gath-ered in the ho - ly place Their voic - es they in worship raise,

Their anthems swell where God doth dwell 'Mid an - gels' songs of praise.

"The Great White Host" (folksong version)—"Den store hvite flokk"—from Lutheran Hymnary.

branches of Norwegian Lutheranism that had not yet been joined together as a single body.

Nevertheless, "low church" Lutherans in the end were not satisfied and brought out a hymnal of their own, *Concordia* (1916), which continued to be used in some Norwegian congregations into the 1960s—a reaction surely to the failure to include much of Norwegian hymnody in the *Service Book and Hymnal* of 1958. *Concordia*, which had appeared in a revised and enlarged edition in 1932, was less careful to avoid the kind of sentimental and popular Pietist hymns that had been rejected by the compilers of the *Lutheran Hymnary* as being trivial.

The activities of the Norwegian Lutheran churches in Michigan were not, however, confined to their religious services, which usually meant the

Religion at Home

In the home, religious observance varied, ranging from daily prayers before meals and at bedtime along with frequent Bible reading, to none at all in secular households. The usual table prayer that everyone knew was:

I Jesu navn går vi til bords	In Jesus' name go we to the table
Å spise og drikke på dit ord,	To eat and drink according to his Word,
Deg Gud til ære, oss til gavn:	To God the honor, us the gain:
Så får vi mat, i Jesu navn. Amen.	So we have food, in Jesus' name. Amen.

In observant households, the recitation of the Lord's Prayer was common, and in free-church families, ex tempore prayers were popular.

A common prayer spoken by children at bedtime after the change to the English language is one that would hardly be advised today:

> *Now I lay me down to sleep.*
> *I pray the Lord my soul to keep.*
> *If I should die before I wake,*
> *I pray the Lord my soul to take.*
> *Amen.*

If it suggests the superstitious belief that evil lurked in the air after the setting of the sun, this prayer in that sense is a protection against the powers of darkness.* However, it also reflects anxiety about the fragility of life, especially among children. Prior to the introduction of antibiotics, and in remote areas without nearby medical care, people, especially the young, were much more susceptible to death from accident and disease. But separated from their home country and often living in small, isolated Norwegian American communities, closeness to God was for so many a consolation that made life endurable and even a joy.

* It has been reported that long ago in Norway, people sometimes took sharp metal objects to bed at night as protection against evil spirits. See also the alignment of "night's dark" with "danger," for example, in the hymn "Awake, thou that sleepest" (*Lutheran Hymnary*, no. 159).

shortened version of the Mass as introduced by Luther, with Communion being celebrated once a month at most, but in both kinds, the bread and the wine. As the social center of the Norwegian community, the churches were famous for women's organizations (ladies' aids), church dinners, and similar functions. But they also served an important educational function, at first helping to keep the Norwegian language alive and also providing instruction in other subjects. Confirmation classes were universal, since this rite was considered necessary for entrance into adulthood and for admission to the Communion table. Sometimes the latter heavily emphasized the rote learning of the *Luther's Small Catechism* and other doctrinal formulae, as well as, of course, the Ten Commandments, the Lord's Prayer, and the Apostles' Creed.

There was also very early concern for missions and charitable projects, efforts the need for which had been learned by practical experience in America. Such habits of charitable behavior would eventually be channeled toward relief for Norway during World War II, as surveyed elsewhere in the present book. It can hardly be said that the Norwegians were insular in their outlook. Yet it is surprising that in early years, except where their ethnic churches were not available, Norwegians tended to remain separate from, for example, other Scandinavians or Germans of the Lutheran tradition. On the other hand, those Norwegians who left the Lutheran Church were more immediately exposed to other ethnic groups and thus became more quickly assimilated into the American culture.

Household prayer was important in daily life, but one consolation was denied most Norwegian Americans, and that was praying to the Virgin Mary or to the saints. Nevertheless, one saint remained in the Norwegian consciousness, though he was not normally invoked by believers. This was St. Olaf Haroldson, Norway's patron saint. It is no surprise that his name was to be given to St. Olaf College in Minnesota, the premier institution of higher education among Norwegian Americans. As an officially Protestant country, Norway had distanced itself from the cult of this saint in the sixteenth century. His relics were removed, and travel along the old pilgrim routes, especially from Oslo and other locations in Scandinavia to his shrine at Nidarøs (that is, modern Trondheim), was discontinued. It was said that at his initial place of burial, a spring emerged from the ground, flowing with healing water. If memory of this miracle was lost after the Reformation, it was

St. Olaf

St. Olaf's story is told by Snorre Sturlason in the *Olaf Saga*, and his conversion is celebrated in a folk song, "Hellig Olaf," included in the *Sons of Norway Song Book*, where it is translated thus:

> *Sainted Olaf, while the flowers of mead and wood*
> *Through the snow were shyly peering,*
> *With his army once upon the fjord-side stood*
> *Pentecost was swiftly nearing.*
> *Mirrored lay his dragon [ship] close behind the strand,*
> *Near him stood the bishop, holy cross in hand,*
> *Fell the heroes there*
>
> *On their knees in prayer,*
> *Solemn awe over all appearing.*
>
> *Sainted Olaf's face did glow with heavenly light,*
> *On his brows his crown was beaming;*
> *Carpet-like his purple robe, majestic, bright,*
> *Over the sand was grandly streaming.*
> *And a church to build had Olaf pledged his word,*
> *There to worship Christ the mighty one, the Lord,*
> *All on Whitsuntide, from its roof should wide*
> *Over the strand its cross be gleaming.*

* Trans. Auber Forestier, in *Sons of Norway Song Book* (Minneapolis: Supreme Lodge of the Sons of Norway, 1948), 115 (slightly modified).

never forgotten that he was the Norwegian king who brought Christianity to the land. Regarded as a martyr, he was killed at the battle of Stiklestad on July 29, 1030, a day remembered as a major feast day in Norway for five hundred years.

As a patriot saint, Olaf was honored not only for his contribution to the religious life of Norway but also for establishing peace and justice in the kingdom. He had a reputation of maintaining honesty and standing against widespread bribery and corruption that had been previously present in the state. These remained essential Norwegian values throughout history thereafter, albeit not always maintained. However, in enforcing Christianity, St. Olaf used harsh methods when persuasion did not succeed, as was customary in those days.

St. Olaf's popularity was not confined to Scandinavia, but was spread through the regions in England where Norwegians had come to work and trade. For example, in York, where, as noted above, Norwegian influence and even political control were present, there is a church named after him as patron, and this is not an isolated instance in the British Isles.

Since Norwegian history was not taught in Michigan, few children who attended the "common schools"—that is, public schools—would have learned more than the rudiments of Olaf's accomplishments, if indeed that. Olaf's early life was colorful and hardly what we would expect of a saint, for he had been a pirate and warrior who was active from the Baltic to Normandy, the latter the location where he was converted to Christianity.

Other Norwegian saints, like St. Sunniva of Bergen, are largely forgotten both in the Old Country and in the New World. Very few Norwegian Americans converted to Roman Catholicism, largely because of the wall of separation that this denomination built against those not within its control. The feeling of superiority of Norwegian Americans toward the Irish, especially Irish Catholics who were also recent arrivals, was an additional factor.

The Music of Norwegian Americans

An elderly lady from Michigan reported that her grandfather, Peter Auensen, owned a "Victrola," or mechanical phonograph that did not require electricity, and she remembers a recording he played that expressed his nostalgia for the Old Country. She identified the song as "I'll Return to Norway." This most likely, of course, was the translation of the title of a song sung in Norwegian. Such songs were part of a flowering of Scandinavian-American pop repertoire that sprang up at the end of the nineteenth century in areas more heavily populated with Scandinavians, with the Cedar Avenue district of Minneapolis being a center. Here, dance bands made up of both Norwegians and Swedes flourished, and their music was widely distributed throughout all the ethnic communities in the Midwest both by oral tradition and through printed scores—and, of course, from 78 rpm wax disk recordings played on the wind-up phonograph.

Music of this kind is distinct from that which was played and sung in Norway, in part because many regional differences had already been more or less erased. Increasingly, Norwegian and Swedish tended to merge in new American pan-Scandinavian cultural production. As studied by ethnomusicologist LeRoy Larson, who has made the study and revival of this "Old Time" music his life's work, the result was a mix of folk songs, dialect songs, waltzes, polkas, and schottisches.[123]

In spite of interest elsewhere, including Norway itself, in Michigan most of this music has long ago lost its appeal, except as an occasional airing on Garrison Keillor's radio program *Prairie Home Companion*, which, incidentally, has hosted Larson's Minnesota Scandinavian Ensemble many times. The decline was accelerated by those cultural forces that encouraged the accessing of outside mainstream entertainment, and by the increasing fragmentation of the formerly tightly knit Norwegian communities.

Aside from the areas in Norway where the Hardanger fiddle predominated, the modern violin was the principal instrument used to play folk music. When coming to America, immigrant players of the violin had another advantage, for these were instruments that were portable and could be packed away with their luggage when they left the home country. Other native instruments such as the *langeleik*, a stringed instrument that has been described "as cross between zither and a dulcimer," and pipes and horns seem to have been left behind or else have failed to receive notice in Michigan.[124] The heritage music noted above, however, has added other instruments, including the accordion, concertina, piano, guitar, string bass, and even banjo, the latter a typically American invention. What this demonstrates is a further dimension of acculturation as the music both encountered the ethnic diversity within the Scandinavian-American community and also experienced the influence of the larger American pop music scene.

With the decline, the old days that had been special for music and dance also disappeared. It has not been possible to ascertain whether immigrants who arrived in Michigan in the nineteenth century celebrated Midsummer with a maypole and dancing, as was the case in some other regions in the Midwest. The tradition of Midsummer, while strong in Norway and remaining the last great pagan festival, seems not to have been celebrated very much in America after the beginning of the twentieth century, in any case. Even *Syttende Mai* as an occasion for festivities could not be maintained in the more sparsely populated Norwegian communities in Michigan.

Also lost over time were visits to many communities in the state by itinerant musicians and entertainers—such as the second-generation Norwegian American Daniel Aakhus, who traveled from his base in Minnesota around the Midwest with his wife Gecina to perform, sometimes on long tours away from home and sleeping either in their car or in a tent.[125] Gecina was a talented entertainer who sang to piano accompaniment and was a gifted

The Hardanger Fiddle

This beautifully constructed instrument, with inlay of mother of pearl, differs from the ordinary modern violin by having gut strings and, importantly, four, or sometimes five, sympathetic metal strings under the fingerboard. Its ancestors were in part the ancient Norwegian *fidla* and *gigja* as well as the viola d'amore. Its tuning varied, including one system that is known as "troll" tuning: A, E♯, A♯, C♯♯ on the main (stopped) strings, and, for the sympathetic strings, C♯, E♯, F♯, and A♯. As Hans Jørgen Holman notes, its "music is highly ornamented and generally is in two voice-parts in addition to the drone effect produced by the sympathetic strings," commonly makes use of dissonance, and is highly sophisticated in its use of overtones.

Hardanger fiddles displayed by Karin Løberg Code and David Code to show the elaborate inlay and decorative work as well as the double set of strings. Each wears a bunad. The man's bunad includes a checked wool vest with a stand-up collar. Photo courtesy of Karin and David Code.

The repertoire includes more than a thousand *slaatter*, some in duple and others in triple time. One of the most important is the bridal march (*bruremarsj*).*

* Hans Jørgen Holman, "Hardingfele, Hardanger Fiddle," in Willi Apel, *Harvard Dictionary of Music*, 2nd ed. (Cambridge, MA: Harvard University Press, 1969), 366; Nils Grinde, *A History of Norwegian Music*, trans. Halverson and Sateren (Lincoln: University of Nebraska Press, 1991), 91–103; Great Lakes Folk Festival website, *http://glff2004.greatlakesfolkfest.net/Programs&Activities*, accessed January 15, 2009.

storyteller. Even their two children, Thelma ("Babe") and Donovan, were involved when not in school; they joined in the performances by dancing traditional dances and playing the piano. Appearing in churches, schools, and halls, their concerts, which included classical as well as Norwegian melodies, were very well attended, and reviews were enthusiastic. In 1925 the Aakhus Concert Company disbanded. This was a critical decade for Norwegian music in this country.

In Norwegian folk music at present, the most interesting development, which dates from the 1980s, is the resurgence of the Hardanger fiddle (*hardingfele*), originally associated with the coastal area between Hardanger and Sunnfjord and with Valdres, Hallingdal, and Telemark. At one time there were many immigrants who played this instrument, but few of the second generation followed in their parents' footsteps. Before the period of resurgence, estimated numbers of players dwindled to probably no more than a score in the whole country. Now there is an active Hardanger Fiddle Association of America that promotes the art of playing this instrument. A periodical, *The Soundpost*, has been published quarterly since 1984.[126]

Michigan has a very highly respected Hardanger fiddle player and teacher, Karin Løberg Code, who not only has studied extensively in Norway but also has been recognized there as a master of this instrument. Code notes that "the Hardanger fiddle's rich and complicated music makes it a real challenge to play. For the musician to play the melody and harmony at the same time can seem an impossible task, but it all works into a beautiful woven texture."[127] She has appeared on Norwegian State Radio and Radio Norway International. With her husband David Code, also a Hardanger fiddle player, she has given concerts in Michigan and elsewhere in the States. Their children have also learned Norwegian dances and have appeared with their parents, all of them in Norwegian *bunader* (costumes).

The music surveyed above is mainly audience-oriented, but of course could also be communal, especially when performed in a family or school setting. Much of it may be classified as entertainment. However, like church music, it could serve to promote solidarity in the Norwegian community at the same time that, when played or sung within the family or with friends, it was a marker of ethnic identity. As such it was an important dimension of Norwegian American life.

In addition to popular secular music in this context, the possibilities for the remainder could be divided into two categories: traditional ballads and religious folk songs. Information about the former in Michigan is lacking, and it has been suggested that ballads did not travel well over the Atlantic.[128] However, the latter category certainly did play a major role in many Norwegian American homes, as they had in Norway, where they constituted the largest single category of vocal music in the Norwegian folk repertoire.[129] Some of these songs, particularly in Pietist families, might differ considerably

Norwegian Repertoire

Detroit was one of the cities visited by the Norwegian Royal University Chorus on its second tour of the United States in 1939. In this concert, the musicians maintained an entirely Norwegian repertoire, including classical works by Edvard Grieg, Christian Sinding, and others—most interestingly, perhaps, Halfdan Kjerulf's "Bridal Procession in Hardanger" ("Brudeferden i Hardanger"), which in its use of folk-dance material is regarded as a forerunner of Grieg's *Norwegian Peasant Dances*, and F. A. Reissiger's "Olaf Trygvason."* The latter is a ballad by Bjornstjerne Bjornson of the death of a national hero, a Viking king who died in battle in 1000 C.E. during a naval battle against the Danes, with Olav's Viking longship being designated as an "Ormen lange" ("long serpent"). Its refrain "Where is that great Long Serpent? / Cometh never Olaf Tragvason" is altered, to reflect Olaf's misfortune, to "Taken is the great Long Serpent, / Fallen is Olaf Trygvason" in the final two stanzas.

The next section of this Detroit concert was comprised of Norwegian folk-song arrangements, beginning with Grieg's amusing "Norwegian Dance" ("Springdans"), to the words (in translation):

> When I go out in an evening
> And meet a friend,
> I want to have a drink.
> When I am quite drunk,
> I fall in a heap,
> And they leave me lying there.†

There is unfortunately no evidence that, with the possible exception of Grieg, the repertoire of this concert was an influence on music chosen for Michigan concerts by Michigan artists subsequently.

* From the concert program, kindly supplied by Larry Syndergaard. The song by Kjerulf and the folk song about Olaf Trygvason are included, with translations of the texts, in the *Sons of Norway Song Book* (Minneapolis: Supreme Lodge of the Sons of Norway, 1948), 80–81, 115.
† Translation from the concert program notes.

from the repertoire and style of hymns sung in church, and the rule was the prevalence of local traditions that varied widely across the country. Further, performance implied improvisation, which would mean that different performances by the same performers would themselves inevitably differ. In spite of the pressures that have been noted earlier on older traditions throughout the 1920s, many favorite religious songs that had sustained the previous generations, still sung with their Norwegian texts, did not instantly disappear, in spite of the omission of the original words from the new Lutheran hymnals and the inevitable change to English for the liturgy. Of course as time went on, these songs too faded from the Norwegian American consciousness, with the late 1940s being more or less their final years.

With the improvement in transoceanic travel in the twentieth century, there was a considerable amount of cultural exchange, as when Detroit's Scandinavian Symphony visited and performed in Norway and the other Nordic countries in 1950. Over the years, many music groups in turn came to the United States to showcase standard and Norwegian repertoire.

A typical postwar tour was the Sandefjord Girl's Choir, which performed in Michigan at Berrien Springs and Detroit in 1976. Their repertoire was mostly standard European art music, but with a few pieces by such Norwegians as Knut Nystedt and Egil Hovland added. On the lighter side, for example, the talented crossover soprano Sissel Kyrkjebø visited as part of a tour connected with promoting Public Broadcasting in 2008, while the Tord Gustavsen Trio made two stops in Michigan, at Ann Arbor and Kalamazoo, in its 2008–09 North American tour. The latter ensemble makes use of Scandinavian folk music, but combined with jazz, blues, hymns, Caribbean music, and other popular and classical forms.

A frequent visitor to Michigan since winning the Kalamazoo-based Irving Gilmore International Piano Festival award in 1998 is Norwegian pianist Leif Ove Andsnes, who is especially noted for his performances of the music of Edvard Grieg.

Arts and Crafts

Norway had a tradition of folk arts from very early times. Carvings from the first millennium C.E. show a vitality that surprises and delights. Medieval Christian carvings such as those on stave churches, some of them eight hundred years old, are considered masterful, and rightly so. Elaborate carving both inside and on the exterior of the churches—decorated timbers and doorways, crucifixes like the famous thirteenth-century example at Røldal that was venerated into the nineteenth century, and large dragon figures extending from the roofs—are still there to surprise the visitor from America.[130]

Carving had continued as a craft up to the time of emigration and was carried to the New World. The techniques and style of carving found in items brought to Michigan by Norwegian immigrants, however, were postmedieval developments. In the eighteenth century, the fashion for using acanthus designs borrowed from the Baroque became prevalent, and this influenced not only later folk carving but also other arts.[131] In the nineteenth century, the technique that was most prevalent was chip carving, a practice identified with the work of Herman Soli from Østfold (1894–1977). He was a laborer and sailor on his first sojourn in Michigan, but later returned and did woodcarving as a sideline to other work, apparently never on a commercial basis.[132] Others who practiced carving may well have come to the state, or worked on the sailing ships on the Great Lakes, before him.

Many Norwegian men, however, had acquired considerable ability in carpentry and in related carving skills in the Old Country. These skills were put to use making the carved altarpiece frames of churches, such as the examples at the Norwegian Lutheran church at Calumet, Bethany Lutheran Church at Northport, and other locations in the state. The frames that still exist demonstrate a sensitivity to design and a particularly Norwegian adaptation of the columns, spires, and pillars of the Gothic Revival. Unfortunately, some of the frames were painted white or varnished, whereas originally they were of uncolored natural wood.[133]

Many carved objects still appear in the possession of families of Norwegian American descent. Among those that were brought from Norway are many humbler items not necessarily elaborate in design—for example, snuff boxes, ideally made from bone. These nevertheless required careful workmanship. It is not always possible to ascertain whether some boxes were created for this tobacco product or for some other purpose, as in the case of small rectangular boxes with hinged covers. Bone boxes of the latter type might be unpainted, but with a small and simply crafted piece of silver fitted into the cover.

Painted objects were more usual. Norwegians often arrived in America with elaborately painted sea chests and a supply of national dress, which were distinctive markers of the various regions from which they had come and also of their social class. The chests, which held the immigrants' belongings, have become valued acquisitions by American folk museums such as Vesterheim in Iowa. Of course, whether painted or not, they were necessary for the family's sea travel to this country, not only for clothing but also for supplies needed while crossing the ocean. Even plain sea chests were likely to be retained as family possessions for generations.

The clothing brought from rural regions in Norway included everyday wear and what we might call "Sunday best." In the case of women, clothes had distinguished single, married, or widowed status, though of course to the Americans whom they encountered they simply seemed exotic and primitive—or absurd, since they represented nonconformity. Social pressures were a factor, and immigrants quite quickly adapted, with men giving up their knee breeches upon arrival. Norwegian styles, however, were often not fully put aside. Remnants of Norwegian design are seen in photos of confirmands and marriage parties into the twentieth century.[134] Except in

A Norwegian Sunday School class c. 1900 at Frenchtown, Quincy Mining Company. The children and adults are dressed in their "Sunday best." Photo courtesy of Michigan Technical University Historical Collections.

exceptionally low-church or Pietist circles, Lutheran pastors continued to wear some article of clothing to distinguish them as clergy, and for church services they often retained the cassock and black stole as well as the elaborate white ruff worn about the neck, though eventually they chose to wear the same vestments as other Lutheran clergymen in America. The Pietists, as for example in Norwegian Lutheran Free Church circles, rejected all liturgical vestments and appeared at the altar in business suits or "Sunday best."[135]

At traditional weddings, when the bride also wore a bridal crown and a special embroidered bib, her colorful *bunad* could be a masterpiece of the dressmaker's art.[136] Christenings, confirmation, and Christmas day were also occasions for dressing in one's very best, while church-going always demanded that one put aside one's everyday clothes. *Bunader* likewise were associated with Norwegian folk dancing, for colorful clothing was part of the spectacle in Norwegian and Norwegian American communities alike. In America, *bunader* brought from Norway were usually not discarded but rather put away. They could still be brought out for special events. Among

Sølje, a silver brooch of the type worn on their bunader by Norwegian women. Photo: Dennis Darling.

early immigrants, bridal dresses, even if not worn for many years, might be retained for use as one's funeral attire, felt to be appropriate for the end of life.

A woman's *bunad*, created from differing fabrics and elaborately embroidered, naturally involved considerable expense, even for the woman who made her own. Today a *bunad*, including all the accessories, can still cost a considerable sum. In America, where the garment is more likely than not worn only at ethnic functions such as meetings of the Sons of Norway, the design may be more or less a standard national dress derived from the design associated with the Hardanger area, rather than a reflection of folk tradition from the region of one's great grandparents.

The most valuable of the accessories worn on the *bunad* was the *sølje*, or silver brooch, which again originally was unique to the region of Norway from which the woman would have come. These were elaborate pendants with dozens of small and delicate silver dangles, a spectacular miniature work of Norwegian silversmiths.

Embroidery was an important part of the design of the apron that was worn with the *bunad*, but was also frequently practiced on such humble articles as pillowcases or dishtowels. Tablecloths, napkins, and curtains also were often decorated with embroidery. Initially the women followed designs from their homeland, but some second-generation Norwegian Americans began to copy inferior American embroidery patterns that could be obtained commercially. In this, they also used embroidery thread purchased at the local dry-goods store, and thus the natural dyes were abandoned for standardized colors according to what was available. The craft was generally abandoned by the subsequent generations of more acculturated Norwegian Americans born in the twentieth century.

However, knit goods are still popular. Norwegian sweaters are very much prized, and heritage shops do a brisk business in this merchandise. In spite of their cost, they are valued not only by persons of Norwegian descent, but by many in the general public for their warmth and durability. Some Norwegian American women still knit them according to the traditional techniques and patterns that have been developed and passed on over the past 150 years.

Grace Strong, located at Marquette, uses a knitting machine to produce Norwegian sweaters that she widely markets. Having discovered that knitting machines had been used in Norway as early as 1589, she has joined the efficiency of technology with a passion for quality and authenticity. She uses Merino Ramboullet wool yarn, from sheep grown in Allegan County, exclusively for her sweaters.

Weaving was universally practiced in Norwegian society from the earliest times in the Old Country and was considered to be the "national craft." In the cold Michigan climate, the weaving of coverlets supplied a real need. However, by the 1920s, "advanced" weaving was reported to be nearly a lost art in America.[137] Weaving nevertheless died away slowly, at the last being confined to small throw rugs that did not require a loom. These also might be made from rags, pieces from worn-out clothing that had been frugally retained. Similarly, very attractive braided rugs, usually formed into an oval shape, were also made from such scraps of cloth.

Knitting

Knitting (*strikking*) using two colors of yarn is not as old as might be suspected. This method of knitting has been attributed to the inventiveness of a milkmaid named Marit Emstad, who first produced two-color knitted mittens around 1855. Single-needle *nålbinding* had been known since the Bronze Age, but in spite of subsequent advances, the fashioning of the well-known modern sweaters required the development of a way of knitting in the round, either with several needles, usually five, or a one-piece needle designed to facilitate this process. *Setesdalsgenser*, or sweaters from the area of Setesdal in southern Norway, are especially liked for their bold design. In Norway these are also called *lusekufte*, meaning "lice jacket," referring to the pattern of white spots in the design. It became usual to add figures, such as reindeer or geometrical shapes, across the yoke and on the sleeves and cuffs.* While originally sweaters were made from undyed wool, with the introduction of dyes and the two-color technique each design came to signify a different region in Norway. Some fishermen's sweaters combined natural wool below with the design appearing only on the upper part, since that was the portion exposed above the overalls worn by men engaging in this occupation.

* A very good general introduction to Norwegian knitting is Rebecca Ganzel, "Strikking: Knitting Wins Hands Down as Norway's National Handicraft," *Sons of Norway Viking* (November 1994): 13ff; but especially see the well-respected guide by Sheila MacGregor, *Traditional Scandinavian Knitting* (Mineola, NY: Dover Publications, 1984), esp. 40–61.

Another use for scraps of cloth, leftovers from sewing dresses or other articles of clothing, was the creation of quilts, which sometimes were highly artistic in spite of the humble materials from which they were made. Pieces were cut to size, basted, and then sewn, using careful backstitching. Cheap ready-made clothing eventually replaced the clothes that had been painstakingly sewn by the women of the household, at first by hand and then with a foot-pedal sewing machine. But after the arrival of synthetic fibers, all salvaged cloth tended simply to be discarded as Norwegian Americans joined in the throwaway culture of their adopted land.

Wall paintings, popular in churches and sometimes too in houses throughout Scandinavia, appear in Michigan in at least one instance—the previously mentioned painting over the apse in the Norwegian church at

Calumet, where there is also a typical reredos painting on canvas. The norm for the latter generally followed a rather stereotyped pattern. The scenes typically depicted Jesus in a white gown, standing and often reaching out to one or more of the disciples. Their intent was to emphasize Jesus' love for humankind. These were mostly painted by Midwestern immigrants, many of them from what may be called the "Minneapolis School," and replicated designs found in engravings in religious books from Scandinavia and Germany. Beneath the painting, on the altar predella, the following words often appeared: "Herre frels mig" ("Lord, save me").[138]

However, rosemaling, the decorative painting that appeared on chests and other objects such as bowls, plates, boxes, and breadboards, has fared better. Rosemaling arose in the eighteenth century, again in distinctive forms in different regions, and remained popular until the latter part of the nineteenth century, at which time the influence of the new manufacturing techniques and the availability of new and easily purchased (but inferior) kinds of paint, and the difficulty in finding traditional pigments, meant a decline of quality here as well. Its revival in America has been linked to Per Lysne, who began painting in his own style in the Depression era and is regarded as the father of modern rosemaling in America. His style was unique, still copied by rosemaling painters, and was characterized by flowers not connected with each other and on the whole most reminiscent of the Os style. Today, rosemaling is recognized as a very distinctive art form that is, at its best, highly valued.[139]

Rosemaling technique is distantly descended from early Norwegian interlace design such as that seen in carvings in stave churches, or even earlier in remnants of Viking art. It also was deeply influenced by later carving styles, in particular the leaf and flower designs of the Baroque. Interlace scrolls are commonly encountered, often in the form of acanthus leaves. The appearance of the acanthus leaf is in itself interesting, since this form was an import from southern Europe that was used in the art of the aristocracy, while rosemaling is very much a folk art. The appearance of flowers also has a connection with baroque paintings.

Practitioners in Norway were generally poor men who had taken up the craft of itinerant painter, working mainly for well-off landed farmers. The art was thus not easily transplanted to Michigan, with its sparse population of Norwegians, who were widely separated in different regions of the state.

Rosemaling

The art of rosemaling involves applying decoration to a smooth painted wood surface, which forms the background against which brilliant color emerges. The surface may be flat or curved, as in the case of painted bowls or plates. One color dominates, but always a careful balance is maintained. The dominant color may be red, blue, green, or gold. Color charts, materials required, and discussions of technique are now widely available. The best introduction in English may be Margaret M. Miller and Sigmund Aaseth, *Norwegian Rosemaling: Decorative Painting*

However, especially since the 1960s, there has been a remarkable revival of the art in America that has affected artists working in this tradition in Michigan. Pat Virch of Marquette has not only become a recognized painter but has written several useful guides to the art of rosemaling,[140] and practitioners are also located in Detroit and southwest Michigan. Some have traveled from Michigan to attend classes at the Vesterheim Museum in Decorah, Iowa, or to take advantage of other opportunities for study. Rosemaling, as it appears on various household goods, has become popular on products that may be designated heritage items—even mailboxes.

Photo, left: Examples of contemporary rosemaling by members of the Askeladden Rosemaling group. Center box, Valdres style (Joyce Hare); from bottom, clockwise: breadboard, Rogaland style (Louise Adams); bowl, Rogaland style (Bea Peterson); plate, Telemark style (Joyce Hare); plate, Per Lysne, adaptation of Os style (Louise Adams); plate, adaptation of Telemark style (Louise Adams); set of boxes, Rogaland style (Jan Christianson). Photo: Gary Yonkers.

on Wood (1974).[*] Oil paints are still used, though for health reasons many prefer to work with acrylic colors. While it is common for contemporary painters to use preexisting patterns, master rosemaling painters work free-hand in painting their scroll designs, in which C and S shapes may predominate. In this way, originality is assured, with each painted object having its own uniqueness. Brush strokes must be applied in certain ways, including carefully calculated pressure, to create the effect desired from the scroll designs. In creating flower designs, each petal must be made with a single stroke of the brush. Such designs will vary from one region of Norway to another, with the regions of Telemark, Valdres, Hallingdal, and Gudbrandsdalen providing the most dominant forms of the art. However, for those who are reviving the art, a choice may be made from all the options available. When finished, a glaze may be applied to the painting,

[*] A color wheel published by Tru-Color Systems of Danville, IN, has forty-two colors used in rosemaling painting and also has a guide to mixing paint to achieve them. A useful introduction to rosemaling technique, albeit quite brief, appears in Jo Sonja Jansen, *Jo Sonja's Guide to Decorative Painting* (New York: Watson-Guptill Publications, 1999), 158–63, 244–49.

Folklore, Superstitions, and Humor

The best known figure in Norwegian folklore is the troll. This unpleasant creature, a dweller under hills or in caves, was once the centerpiece of stories about Norway told to children of Norwegian descent, and currently a commercial variant of this creature has entered the realm of pop culture. Upper Peninsula residents call people from the lower part of the state "trolls" since they live below the Mackinac Bridge which crosses the straits between Lake Michigan and Lake Huron.

Folklore involves an oral tradition in which stories may emerge in different forms, sometimes slightly so, sometimes radically so. Sometimes the parts are interchangeable. So folklorists in Norway have recorded a story about St. Olaf and a troll that is remarkably like the example that will be presented here. This is not an example that has specifically been recorded in Michigan, but it nevertheless demonstrates the type of folk tale that circulated among the earliest Norwegians to come to the state. A troll offered to help a man to build a church. However, if by the conclusion of the project the man could not tell his name, the troll would be rewarded with his eyes and his heart. When only a portion of a support column for the church remained, the man still had not learned the troll's name. Fortunately, as he stepped away to find some rest on a bank, he heard the troll's wife singing a ballad in which she was bragging that tomorrow she would be rewarded

Askeladden

The following is an example that may be regarded as more or less typical of the Askeladden stories:

> After the death of their father, the two elder brothers and the ashlad, the youngest, go to work in the palace, with Askeladden given the task of washing pots and pans in the kitchen. However, he is well liked, compared to his clumsy brothers. A troll's seven silver swans swim on a nearby lake. The elder brothers go to the king to say that Askeladden has bragged that he could capture them. He denies this. But he will give it a try. He has brought with him a large kneading pan in which he will set out. He brings with him a supply of wheat and rye by which he will coax the silver swans to him, whereupon he returns to the king with them.
>
> Next the elder brothers again plot against Askeladden, in this instance by telling the king that he has promised to come away with the troll's bed quilt, which is decorated with gold and silver patches. Again he denies this, but after some thought he will set out once more across the lake. The troll has his bed quilt out to air in the sun at just this time, so Askeladden luckily is able to snatch it away and row off in the kneading trough. The feat so impresses the king that Askeladden is promoted to be his personal servant. The jealous elder brothers make one more attempt. They arrange that the king should hear that Askeladden has promised to steal away the troll's golden harp. As a

with his body parts by Fin. The man then returned, called Fin by name, and saw him fly away in anger with the portion of stone pillar.[141] In other stories, as we would expect, the troll is successful, and sometimes trolls are treated with benign familiarity, as when Edvard Grieg, the great nineteenth-century Norwegian composer, gave the name of Troldhaugen (Troll Hill) to his house near Bergen.

In appearance, the troll was said to be very ugly, sometimes one-eyed or with a large misshapen nose. He was clever, but defective in logical reasoning. Like the invisible *huldre* folk who lived underground, he could be the source of evil and misfortune. Both had dark and sour dispositions, and hence vivid stories were easily created that demonstrated their reward, the king offers him the princess and half of the kingdom. Once more he denies that he has made any such promise, but after some days of thinking about it, he sets off in his kneading trough carrying a large nail, a birch stick, and a candle. The troll catches him, puts him in a fattening cage, and tells his daughter they will get him ready for a feast. However, after eight days, when his daughter tests him to see if he is fat enough, he holds out the nail, which she is not able to cut. The next time, again after eight days, it is the stick of birch, which impresses the troll's daughter that progress is being made in fattening him up. The final time, the same number of days later, he holds out the candle, which she cuts into easily. The troll sets out to invite the guests, and she begins to prepare the knife with which she is to take his life. She sharpens and sharpens. Askeladden offers to help sharpen the knife for her, then turns on her and cuts off her head preparatory to cooking her for the feast. Dressing himself in her clothes and playing on the harp, he will deceive the troll upon his return and will escape with it in his kneading trough. During each of these adventures Askeladden taunts the troll, and at the end, of course, gets to marry the princess and receive half the kingdom. Finally, he is generous to his elder brothers, for he believes only good of them and imagines they had his best interests in mind throughout.*

* This retelling preserves the basic contour of the folktale from George Webbe Dasent, *Popular Tales from the Norse* (Edinburgh: David Douglas, 1888), 215–21.

undesirability. An example, concerning *huldre* folk, who in contrast to trolls are described as spirits, is given by Reidar Christiansen:

At a farm, husband and wife were always quarreling. One day, during a meal, they kept on their usual way, when the door was thrown open and one of those dwellers under the ground looked at them and said, "The same thing here as with us!" And then he slammed the door and vanished.[142]

If such creatures loomed larger in the consciousness in Norway, in this country they could nevertheless serve as incarnations of the boogeyman, long invoked when children were out of line in their behavior.

Stories about a smaller fairy creature called the *nisse*, who was essentially a household or farmyard fairy, were verifiably told in Norwegian American households. He was like a small child in stature, only a foot or two tall, but with the face of a old man and dressed in gray clothing with a red stocking cap. Not naturally mischievous, the *nisse* was usually helpful with household or farmyard chores if anything was amiss or required cleaning after the family had gone to bed. However, these little fairies could be demanding, and unforgiving to families that did not bother to set out food at night, preferably butter or *grøt*.[143] In such cases, the little creatures would cause no end of mischief. One story, known across Northern Europe and reported by a Michigan resident, tells of a family plagued with a large and troublesome band of *nisser* living in their house. They decided to move. But when they were well on the way to their new house in their wagon with all their possessions, the *nisser* popped up from the hay in the wagon and said, "We are coming too."[144]

But among Michigan Norwegian Americans, the claim is that the best-remembered tales are those that concern the ash lad, Askeladden, so called because he sits by the fire and idly thrusts the poker into the ashes and for this is reviled by his two brothers. Variant versions appear that are very like the Cinderella story, for he is the one who gets the princess.

Sometimes it seems hard to ascertain where amusing stories end and actual superstition begins. Influenced by nineteenth-century Pietism, a considerable number of immigrants, mainly women, firmly believed that the devil resided in playing cards. As we have seen, the violin, and especially the Hardanger fiddle, was sometimes regarded as demonic by Norwegian Pietists. LeRoy Larson's great-grandmother, from Sogn, believed that the devil was resident in the violin, and similar beliefs among Michigan Norwegian Americans would have been held, especially by immigrants from the west coast of Norway who were deeply influenced by Haugean views.[145] Daniel Aakhus, whose concert tours into Michigan have already been noted, possessed a violin that was reputed to have been owned by the gypsy Peter Strømsing. This instrument was said to be magical, and supposedly when Strømsing was playing in competition, it could create spells causing the strings on other contestants' instruments to snap and break. On one occasion, when this violin was said to have been set down, it did not stop playing, even though the bow was not touching the strings.[146] Needless to say,

A Norwegian kitchen witch. Courtesy of Michigan State University Museum.

Norwegian Pietists also tended to object to dancing, and in America were the first to join the temperance movement.

On the other hand, some women displayed kitchen witches, figures that reflected a complicated attitude toward the demonic that commonly existed alongside deep Christian piety. Kitchen witches, suspended from the ceiling, were supposed to provide protection for the food prepared in the room. They were about eight or nine inches in height and rode on miniature brooms, and they had pointed hats and garments of rags. Though rare, such figures still may be seen in Norwegian American kitchens in Michigan.

While in the Old Country the supernatural had lurked close by, especially at night and at certain times of the year, New World skepticism concerning

Jokes about Swedes

A whole category of Norwegian jokes directed at the most recent dominant neighbor country, Sweden, followed the immigrants to the New World. Many here will repeat the line "Ten thousand Swedes came through the weeds, looking for one Norwegian," but few can give anything like a reliable explanation of its origin, which is possibly lost in one of history's border wars of long ago. But indubitably, it in part derives from Norway's resentment at being placed under nominal Swedish sovereignty from 1814 to 1905, following the long period of Danish domination that some Norwegians still call the "five hundred years of darkness." Constitution Day, which some of Norwegian descent still commemorate, is celebrated on May 17 (*Syttende Mai*), remembering 1814, not the date of separation from Sweden and the reestablishment of the Norwegian monarchy!

The Swedes, not the Danes who earlier dominated Norway, are the butt of many jokes. For example: "Do you know about the Swede who shot an arrow into the air? He missed." "A Swede, hearing that most accidents happen within five miles of home, made a decision. What did he do? He moved." "When Sweden changed from driving on the left side of the road to the right some years ago, how was the transition effected? They did it in stages. They started with the trucks." Of course, the Swedes can turn most of these jokes against the Norwegians very easily, but not this last.*

* The Lars (pronounced as in *Larson*, not *Larz*) and Lena jokes that represent Norwegians or Swedes as country hicks are said to be identified with the Upper Peninsula; see Jeffrey W. Hancks, *Scandinavians in Michigan* (East Lansing: Michigan State University Press, 2006), 75–76.

such things soon was adopted following immigration. By the twenty-first century, most Norwegian Americans find such beliefs to be more worthy of a chuckle than a shiver of fear.

It is sometimes said that Norwegians lack a sense of humor, but this is hardly true. Their specialty seems to be ethnic jokes directed at outsiders who have tried to dominate them. In fact, during the German occupation under which the country suffered in World War II, jokes were a principal means of maintaining the Resistance, for which Norwegians were famous. Kathleen Stokker's study of the role of jokes during this period cites a large number, of which the following is but one example:

A little boy is sitting on the sidewalk playing with some kittens. A German officer comes along and asks the boy, "Are those kittens you're playing with?" "No," the boy says, "They're Nazis."

Three weeks later the officer comes by again and, seeing the same boy playing with the kittens, says, "Are you still playing with those Nazis?" "No," answers the boy. "They're not Nazis anymore; now their eyes are open!"[147]

One joke, which might be expanded to folk-tale length, involves conscription into the army. Supposedly it is set in the times of domination by Sweden, but the details suggest a later time frame and an American origin. A man, usually said to be an uncle or great-uncle or other ancestor, was being called up for conscription in two weeks. Not wanting to be drafted into an army perceived to be foreign, he wrapped his leg in very smelly cheese (Limburger is usually specified) and made a point of getting it wet and dirty so as to appear infected. When he appeared before the army doctor for his medical examination, the doctor leaned over, sniffed disgustedly, and told the man, "Go home, young man, you don't have long to live." Some of the details, to be sure, suggest that this is an invention based on conscription during World War I, when many Norwegian American men were drafted, but it still is indicative of a general antagonism to military service and regimentation. Attitudes changed during World War II, as expected, on account of the great sympathy for the plight of Norway during the occupation.

Relief for German-Occupied Norway, 1940–45

On April 9, 1939, Inger Thoen, now a Michigan resident, sensed that "something terrible" had happened, and indeed it had. Hitler's forces had invaded Norway, a calamity of major proportions. Shortly thereafter, she and her sister saw a Nazi airplane over Oslo for the first time, "large, black . . . with white swastikas painted on both sides" and coming "in very low over our house." She was surprised to see the pilot, an actual human being, and says that she "must have expected a monster of some sort, maybe a troll."[148] Naturally, the invasion of the land of their fathers was also felt deeply as a matter of concern by Norwegian Americans.

Independent-minded Norwegians had no intention of submitting to the occupiers, and a resistance movement against the occupying force rapidly developed. Highly unpopular moves, such as the order commanding school teachers to join the *Laerersamfund* or Nazi teachers' union and to indoctrinate the young, were largely resisted, and the burning of all books of which the Nazis disapproved—not only of Jewish authors but also of many writers such as Sigrid Undset who were beloved in Norway—only alienated the Norwegian people. Many Norwegians, like Inger Thoen's parents, provided hiding places in their homes for Jews fleeing persecution and death, and in doing so, they risked summary execution by the Nazis.[149] The bishops of the Church of Norway resigned, as did virtually all the priests.

Only a few succumbed to the Nazi belief in Nordic superiority, of the *Übermench*, that had been derived by a twisted and distorted fashion from Friederich Nietzsche, Scandinavian myth, and the music dramas of Richard Wagner. The right-wing political leader and collaborator Vidkun Quisling and the aged Knut Hamsun—the latter, to be sure, a talented novelist—were among the minority of citizens who betrayed the Norwegian ideals of freedom and independence most dear to their countrymen. Americans, and not only those of Norwegian descent, were horrified, and the great soprano Kirsten Flagstad, who had gone back to Norway in 1941 and whose husband for a time had been a member of Quisling's party, remained controversial when she returned after the war to sing at the Metropolitan Opera.

The recalcitrance of the Norwegians led to violent action by the Nazi authorities, who hoped for a docile populace that might accept Nazi ideology, as so many Germans had done. Thousands were arrested, some to be imprisoned or taken to concentration camps in Germany. Torture was routine, including the Chinese water torture, which was slower but reported to be no less terrifying than waterboarding, and the use of vicious and threatening dogs. Joseph Terboven, the Gestapo chief brought in to pacify the Norwegians, was particularly blunt and brutal. He is quoted as saying, "It is relatively unimportant to Germany whether a thousand or ten thousand Norwegians starve to death; we have much greater interests to take care of."[150]

Conditions were indeed terrifying for those families that had been separated at the outset of the war or, especially, when the United States entered into the conflict. The family of Carl Hoff of Auburn Heights, Michigan, was one of these. His wife and three daughters spent the war years in Bergen, virtually out of contact with him. Soldiers took what they wanted from the people and deprived them of radios, which were not permitted. Thus isolated, terrified by Allied bombing, and suffering the deprivations of those years as well as the brutality of the occupying force, the family could only endure until they were reunited at the end of 1945.[151]

Olga Hoff wrote to her husband in Michigan after the end of hostilities to say that she was able to buy eggs for the first time in five years. In another letter, she reported looking at her ration card and noticing that "the last time we had meat was in April of 1942."[152] A letter from Commander Leif Melsom of the U.S. Navy in 1945 described the conditions under which people had suffered. Coffee, always the favorite drink of Norwegians, was unobtainable, and the substitute, made of barley or peas, was "a terrible drink without milk or sugar." Tea was made from apple leaves, surely just as vile. Milk was in short supply, the cattle stocks "decimated." Food had been shipped to Germany for the war effort without consideration of what might be needed in Norway. Bread had to be made from flour and cellulose.[153] Inger Thoen reports that her father lost thirty pounds, her mother perhaps only a little less. To survive, Norwegians had found it necessary to improvise, raising vegetables and sometimes even livestock in their back yards.[154]

Clothing worn by Norwegians was also affected, their appearance consequently signifying their neediness and impoverishment. There were no clothes in the stores, and a card seen in tailors' windows advertised "all kinds of underwear are accepted for repairs."[155] Shoes sometimes had to be repaired with wooden soles. Olga Hoff wrote to her husband in July 1945 that the children were very much in need of clothing, which she directed him to ship to Norway as "used" to avoid the heavy duty on such items. "It is true what you have read in America," she said, "that we have paper shoes and clothes and hand towels. I have paper curtains in one of our rooms."[156] Warm garments and blankets had been confiscated for use by the German army, with the consequence that many Norwegians suffered terribly from the cold in their country. Areas of Finnmark, the northernmost county of Norway, had been leveled in 1944, and there were many internal refugees, estimated at 60,000.

Yet, to the consternation of Norwegian Americans and others sensitive to the plight of Norway's citizens, there was at first strong resistance by the United States government to the provision of aid, a stance influenced by the widespread isolationism in America at that time. In 1935 Congress had passed the Neutrality Act, which was used to restrain contact with warring nations in Europe. Norwegian Americans and others concerned with human rights, however, were not deterred from sending aid to beleaguered Norway. Sadly, they were not always successful. A national organization, American Relief for Norway, was formed, and Michigan played a part in this, though not as visibly as states like Minnesota or Iowa where Norwegians were a larger proportion of the population. This organization collected nearly $138 million across the nation. Between 1941 and 1943, scrap leather from the Hudson Motor Car Company was donated for the purpose of making

The Rev. Walter B. Scarvie, Head of Norwegian Relief in Michigan

In 1947, King Haakon VII of Norway conferred a knighthood on the Rev. Walter B. Scarvie (1898–1995) for his efforts as Michigan Chairman of Norwegian Relief during World War II. Scarvie was made a Knight of St. Olaf with Cross, the highest honor given to civilians. His parishioners decided in 1952 to rename their church, founded in Detroit in 1915 as Den Norske Lutherske Kirke and subsequently known as Salem Lutheran Church. Henceforth it was to be known as St. Olaf Lutheran Church. At his retirement in 1964, Scarvie was lauded for his "promotion of Norwegian cultural and spiritual interests in general"—in other words, for his broad support for Nordic

The Rev. Walter B. Scarvie, Lutheran pastor at Detroit and head of Norwegian relief effort in Michigan during the occupation of Norway. Photo from church newsletter. Courtesy of the Bentley Historical Library, University of Michigan.

heritage. He was a second-generation Norwegian American, whose father came from Telemark and his mother from Hallingdal. After completing his education, he had briefly been a professor of classics and languages at Luther College. St. Olaf Lutheran Church, originally affiliated with the Lutheran Free Church, is now a parish in the Evangelical Lutheran Church of America.*

* Bentley Historical Library, Norse Civic Associations, box 5/557.

leather jackets. Other kinds of garments followed when the leather was no longer available, with labor being donated by the state's Lutheran and other churches. Among those assisting were women at the University of Michigan and Mrs. Henry Ford.

In Detroit, money was solicited in the days and months following the invasion by a newly formed Norwegian American Women's Club, and some was sent to Camp Little Norway, where airmen of the Norwegian Air Force were being trained.[157] Special aid was destined for sailors who manned the Norwegian fleet, which had slipped away from the Nazis. A chapter of

American Relief for Norway was formed, with Walter B. Scarvie as chairman for all of Michigan.[158] In December 1941, special Christmas seals were sold for the support of Norwegian relief.[159] By late in 1942, the Red Cross became involved so that medical supplies might be shipped by sea to England and then on through Sweden, at least to a limited degree. Even this effort tended to be severely frustrated as Swedish planes carrying supplies were shot down or disappeared. Shipments by sea were later successful on at least two occasions. The occupiers insisted that all labeling specifying America as the origin of the medical supplies had to be removed. The Red Cross relaxed its rules so that the drugs could be sold by pharmacies, and the proceeds from the sales were to be directed, sometimes clandestinely, to relief for those most severely affected by the war.[160] Refugees were assisted in fleeing from the country, sometimes in small boats and thereafter across the border to Sweden. Food also reached Norway through Sweden during the conflict, with much greater quantities being shipped by sea after the end of the war.

When it became possible to do so, many Norwegian Americans sent packages of food aid, clothing, and even soap (the B soap that had been distributed during the war was hardly usable) to relatives and friends in the Old Country, and eventually were gratified to learn that Norway once again had become a model democracy and a financially successful land in spite of what the citizens had suffered. Today, Norway has a stronger network of social services than the United States, and its per capita income is one of the highest in the world.

Christmas and All the Trimmings

The Norwegian term for Christmas is *Jul*, derived from Old Norse *Jól*, or "slaughter night," a midwinter festival at which blood sacrifices were offered to the pagan gods. It was King Haakon the Good (d. 960 C.E.) who, according to the sagas, "made a law that the festival of Yule should begin at the same time as the Christmas of the Church, and that every man, under penalty, should brew a meal [measure of malt] into ale, and therewith keep the Yule holy as long as it lasted."[161] Some remnants of the pagan festival were retained in the Christian celebration that triumphed, and feasting was always at the center of the Norwegian celebration of the season of *Jul*.

In Norwegian American communities, anticipation began as early as four Sundays before the festival itself. The calendar identifies this as the period of Advent, or preparation for commemorating the coming of Christ into the world. In Lutheran churches, the color green for the long summer "Trinity" season is exchanged for a more somber purple for stoles and altar frontals. Advent was a period of a very special time of feasting and joy, as many who grew up in Norwegian American families will remember from the period before the present time of blatant commercialism and "conspicuous consumption."[162] To be sure, American customs eventually exerted their influence, and children's expectations would include the receiving of generous gifts. At first these were said to be delivered by *julenissen*, wearing a red stocking cap and more or less a cousin of the jolly Santa Claus of today. His greeting was "Er det noen snille barn her?" ("Are there any well-behaved children here?"). At other times in the season, people might repeat "Nå er det jul igjen, nå er det jul igjen, og jula varer ratt til påske" ("Now it is Christmas again, now it's Christmas again, and Christmas lasts until Easter"). Actually, the usual practice was to observe the twelve days leading up to Epiphany (*Helligtrekongersdag*), the day commemorating the arrival of the Three Holy Kings at the site of the Nativity. Even then, if Norwegian customs were being followed, Christmas might not be entirely over until at least St. Knut's day (January 7)—hence the Old Country saying, "Sant Knut jagar Jula ut" (St. Knut drives out Christmas").[163]

For adult Norwegian Americans in Michigan in earlier times, these weeks before Christmas meant an opportunity for collecting supplies for the Christmas feast. For example, plenty of firewood needed to be prepared for heating and cooking. Logs that had been cut the previous winter now were dry enough to burn, but needed cutting with a saw and then splitting with an ax. The choosing of the most combustible wood to cut up for kindling was important. Until mechanized saws were brought into use, all of this was hard work.

With the coming of December, families could safely do butchering without fear that their meat would spoil. The slaughter of the *julegrissen* (Christmas pig) was a traditional event. Blood sausages might be made from the fresh pig's blood, flour, rice, suet, raisins, sugar, and spices. In making *blod pølse*, a mixture having the consistency of pancake batter was tied into sacks and cooked. *Blodklubb*, made of fresh blood, flour, potatoes, and a little sugar, was boiled—then, as a final stage of preparation, was cut into thick slices and fried. *Lutefisk*, when it was purchased from a merchant, was dried cod from Norway that required soaking for eight days, with the water changed daily. One recipe says it then should be placed in a solution of water (one pint) and potash lye (12 pints) for three days, and finally, soaked in plain water for two days.

Other foods that required preparation in advance include *fattigman*, seasonal bread (either a loaf or rolls), and *lefse*, the latter considered very special. Each piece of *lefse* was about the size of a pancake but very thin, and would be buttered and sprinkled with sugar, then rolled up into a roll. Directions for making *lefse* and some other Norwegian foods are included

Pearl Ingebritson in her kitchen, preparing lefse. Photo: Dennis Darling.

in appendix 5. Other delicacies, such as Norwegian *flatbrød*, thin and un-leavened (now commercially sold as "crispbread"), were often imported. Special cheeses such as *gjetost* (goat cheese) or *primost* (whey cheese) might be included—again, products that usually had to be purchased. Split peas and potatoes would have been at hand for the feast.

Personal hygiene was to be given attention immediately before Christmas Day—for many early Norwegian Americans, on Christmas Eve. All the family needed to take baths. For this, a small galvanized washtub was usually used, with water heated in a copper boiler on the cookstove. Before modern times, the water had to be brought in from the well—a considerable task in itself if the family was very large.

Christmas Day, following attendance at church, the final stages of pre-paring the Christmas meal needed to be done, since these tasks could not be arranged in advance. When a special spiced drink of fruit juice, either alcoholic or nonalcoholic, was to be provided, it required heating—in the early days, on the wood cookstove. Desserts had to be readied—for example, *krumkaker* needed to be filled with whipped cream. Most important, the *lutefisk*, now ready for cooking, was placed in boiling water and salt added. When the water came to a boil, it was ready to be served. It was said that the best *lutefisk* should shiver. Norwegian tradition dictates that it should be eaten with melted butter and peas, along with mashed potatoes and gravy. Outsiders at the table might wish to forgo this delicacy—or so it was regarded among Norwegians, surely in part on account of nostalgia for the Old Country. After the table prayer, the feasting would begin.

The alcoholic or, especially in later years, nonalcoholic beverages were served, the former more and more rare as the temperance movement gathered momentum. The universal drink, however, was coffee, the Norwegian national beverage, which was always required. At the end of the meal, the family and friends would all thank the hostess: "Tak for matte" ("Thanks for the food"), and the leftovers would be put away in a cool place, in later years in an icebox or refrigerator.

In the final weeks before Christmas, schoolchildren prepared programs of little recitations and skits retelling the Nativity, or perhaps traditional stories or legends appropriate to the season, and carols were rehearsed. Public schools, in earlier days not particularly mindful of the separation of church and state, often had their own programs on the evening of the final day of school before Christmas vacation. In the countryside, these were carefully planned so as not to interfere with obligatory evening chores. At the churches, preparations were also made for parallel programs, at first in Norwegian so that older folk could appreciate the event. Before the coming of electrification to rural areas, these were magical events, fondly remembered among Norwegian American families. The candlelit room, the excitement of the season, the elaborate decorations and Christmas tree, and the solemn rows of parents coming to watch were all part of the ambience of the event.

Once introduced to Norwegian Americans, the *Juletre* (Christmas tree) would be taken into the house on Christmas Eve and set up on a base, usually made of two pieces of wood shaped like a cross (*korsformet juletrefot*) that might be seen as a reminder that the Nativity also implied what was to be commemorated in the spring when the next great festival of the Church was

A Christmas Carol

As the singing of songs in the Norwegian language faded into memory, with one notable exception, the standard American and English carols that were almost universally sung formed the repertoire. That exception was the delightful "Jeg er så glad hver julekveld," which continued to be loved even after World War II in some communities.

Jeg er så glad hver ju - le - kveld, for
da ble Je - sus født; da lys - te stjer - nen
som en sol, og eng - ler sang så søtt.

The translation of the first stanza is as follows:

I am so glad each Christmas Eve,
The night when Jesus was born.
Then the star shone forth like the sun,
And angels sang so sweetly.

Though in the style of a folksong, the music was composed by Peder Knudsen in 1859 as a setting of words written the same year by Marie Wexelsen.

celebrated. Christmas trees were introduced in England by Queen Victoria and Prince Albert and had migrated to the New World mainly from there by mid-century—a cultural transfer that was perhaps more influential than the introduction of this festival practice in Norway. It was from their neighbors, in the last half of the nineteenth century, that Norwegian Americans discovered and adopted this custom. But up to World War II, the tree was usually outfitted with a combination of Norwegian and American ornaments: sparking strips of tinsel, colored glass balls, small figures, three-dimensional fold-out paper bells, cookies—some of them in the shape of angels or animals—and at the top, a star. Even after electrification, some maintained the tradition of using small candles instead of electric Christmas tree lights. In homes, the candles would burn on Christmas Eve and then on the subsequent evenings of the season—not inevitably all the way to Twelfth Night or St. Knut's Day. It was always important not to leave lighted candles unattended because of the danger of fire, especially as the season drew toward its close and the tree became more dry. By the time it was removed from the house, there was always a pile of dry pine needles under where the tree had stood. In many families, dancing took place around the tree, usually a simple round dance, before the candles were lit. This was accompanied by the singing of songs and carols, sometimes with a musical instrument such as a violin, accordion, or piano joining in.

Then too, when all the family were seated around, Christmas could be a time of pure magic when the present faded into memories of the distant past as related in the Gospel story; but also, when tales were told, these might tend to erase the boundaries between the real and the legendary. Such tales might be ghost stories, but also in early days folktales of trolls, *huldre* or underground folk, and of course *nisser*. Much of the context of such folk belief seems to have been utterly lost as Michigan Norwegian Americans entered the mainstream American culture.

Over time, the Norwegian American Christmas, emerging from an adult festival that had its roots in medieval traditions, developed into an approximation of the generic American Christmas celebrated by others in Michigan. If *lutefisk* is usually no longer on the table, many of the other delicacies are also missing, except in those families that are especially concerned about maintaining their ethnic heritage. Santa Claus replaced *nisser* in the early twentieth century, in some cases not until well after World War I. Many Norwegian American parents even then tended to disabuse their offspring of belief in this legendary figure, albeit one with his roots in the legend of St. Nicholas, patron of children.

The new customs indeed demanded that Christmas should be more focused on children, with the giving of purchased gifts, toys especially, emphasized. Until the post–World War II years, there was nothing of the frenzy of modern-day gift giving in which young people are presented with an immense array of expensive *things*, including electronic devices and sports paraphernalia. Stockings hung up as symbolic receptacles to receive them, at first adequate to hold the gifts, were not adopted for a great many years. In secular Norwegian American families today, Christmas seems to be most prominently an opportunity to bond with children, who are essentially bribed with the things they are given on this day. Santa Claus is firmly entrenched. For those who are churchgoers, a late Christmas Eve service seems to be the norm in the mainline churches. Christmas trees are put up early and thrown out on December 26, and Christmas music, much of it annoyingly repeated over and over, falls out of favor on the same day only to return the following November. Thus, to a very large degree, Michigan's Norwegian Americans have been absorbed into the dominant culture's way of celebrating Christmas.

As noted above, *lutefisk*, once almost always served at home or in the church suppers for which Norwegians were famous, rarely appears at Christmas in Michigan. Nevertheless, *lutefisk* dinners are still prepared in the Lower Peninsula by the Sons of Norway lodge at Muskegon in January and, during the month of December, by the Norwegian Men's Club in Detroit. While ethnic organizations, relatively small in size, still promote Norwegian heritage, the connection with Old Country customs is otherwise more often than not quite diluted, except among those who are recent immigrants—for example, the members of such groups as the Norwegian Women's Club (LYNG) in the Detroit area—or those who have maintained contact with relatives in Norway.

Nevertheless, there are many who have come to feel that the changes occurring in the course of acculturation took place at a considerable price, even though these Norwegian Americans fail to share the anguish of those first-generation immigrants who experienced so keenly the loss not only of Christmas customs but also of language and traditions generally by their children or grandchildren.

Martin Ulvestad's Survey of Norwegian Settlements in Michigan

artin Ulvestad, in his *Nordmændene i Amerika deres Historie og Rekord* (1907), attempted to give a thorough listing of Norwegian settlements and churches in Michigan, but in spite of traveling about widely in the United States himself, he depended on informants for this state and hence was not reliable in details, as readers will notice. Dates in particular should be regarded as approximate. Nevertheless, his survey is worth notice in spite of what will be seen to be its frequent errors and incompleteness. The following is Ulvestad's list of Michigan counties with a summary of his commentary on each.

Lenawee. Visited by Norwegians in 1833; no permanent settlement.

Muskegon. Immigrants arrived in mid-nineteenth century, first permanent settlement in 1848. First Lutheran church built in state, 1865; three other Lutheran congregations, one Evangelical Free Church, one Methodist, one Baptist in the county.

Manistee. Settlement began in 1851. There were two post offices with Norwegian names: Norway and Arendahl. The first Lutherans at Manistee joined the Norwalk Norwegian Evangelical Lutheran congregation, 1864, with construction of a building in 1868, but this was actually a generic

Scandinavian church. The county also has two Norwegian Lutheran churches or congregations.

Oceana. Norwegians started coming to the county, at first settling at Shelby, in 1856. In the county, the first Norwegian congregation in Michigan was organized, but its church was not built until 1884.

Alpena. A former Norwegian sea captain was the first settler in the city of Alpena, 1861. At that time it was a sawmill and fishing center. Some Norwegians established a community at Lier. There is a post office at Leer [Norw.: Lier]. The county has two Norwegian churches.

Benzie. Isak Peterson, fisherman, settled at Frankfort in 1864. Fishing and farming reported. There are three Lutheran congregations in the county; the first of these is the congregation at Frankfort, established in 1873, with the church erected in 1884.

Houghton. Numerous Norwegians came to Calumet to work in the copper mines in 1865. The initial Lutheran congregation at Quincy was established in 1866; the first Norwegian church built was at Calumet in 1876. In all, the county has three Lutheran congregations and a Methodist congregation. Temperance activity is reported.

Montcalm. Norwegian settlers at Lakeview from 1866, a small community, with a Norwegian Lutheran church served by a priest from Norway. Post office named Amble, possibly a Norwegian name.

Leelanau. Norwegians at Northport in 1867; Norwegian congregation of Our Savior's established 1874; the first Lutheran church to be constructed in the county was at Sutton's Bay in 1885. The county has three other Lutheran congregations.

Marquette. Frederick Braastad was the first Norwegian to arrive, in 1868; he left Marquette City for Ishpeming, where he established a store in 1873 that would become very successful. A large community of Norwegians reported there. A few Norwegians came to Michigamme beginning in 1873. Three Lutheran congregations in the county. Northland post office may carry a Norwegian name.

Antrim. The first Norwegian arrived in Elk Rapids in 1869, followed by others. A Lutheran congregation was established in 1882, a church built in 1885.

Schoolcraft. A very isolated county, without postal service in winter; in summer mail came by ship from Chicago. The first settler and his family came to Manistique in 1871. A Lutheran congregation was established in 1888, church built in 1892.

Delta. First Norwegians settled in 1872, at Stonington. The county produces potatoes and is active in the timber industry. First congregation in county organized at Escanaba in 1888, church built in 1891; now two Lutheran congregations in county.

Baraga. Norwegian settlement in Skanee district from 1870s; first Norwegian arrived at L'Anse in 1876. A Methodist church and a small Lutheran congregation are reported.

Gogebic. The earliest settlers came from Wisconsin in 1885, followed by others who came from Norway. One surviving settler resides in Ironwood; the others who are still alive are in Bessemer. Noted as a mining district. One Norwegian Lutheran church reported.

Mason. Norwegians are concentrated in Ludington, where they are served by a Lutheran church, though some belong to a Methodist or a Baptist congregation.

Alcona. A little settlement of Norwegians around Spruce, the first coming in 1892. The Lutheran congregation dates from 1894; church constructed 1899.

Calhoun. While no Norwegian settlement is reported, at Battle Creek the Adventists produced a Norwegian newspaper, *Evangeliets Sendebud,* as well as periodicals.

Charlevoix. A small settlement at East Jordan, the first immigrant coming in 1887, with a Lutheran congregation established in 1902.

Chippewa. Few settled here, the first, a farmer, coming in 1892 to Sault Ste. Marie.

Menominee. Norwegians are present in the city of Menominee and in the surrounding areas. Two Methodist congregations are reported as well as two Lutheran congregations, with two churches having been built.

Dickinson. Norwegians are reported. There are two churches, one Lutheran, one Adventist. Place names: Norway township, and also a town called Norway.

Grand Traverse. Norwegians came to various parts around the county.

Keweenaw. Some Norwegians reported, no churches.

Mecosta. Few Norwegians, one Norwegian Lutheran congregation.

Appendix 2
Norwegian Heritage

Many Norwegian Americans display something in their homes to identify their ethnic connection to Norway, whether it be a small Norwegian flag, a windsock, or piece of Norwegian pewter. Others have purchased Norwegian sweaters, other articles of ethnic clothing, or pewterware. Troll dolls are favorite items with children. Such products are easily obtainable at numerous websites and at stores throughout the Midwest. Their popularity may be gauged by the success of Punzel, an outlet for Scandinavian heritage items located on a remote county road near Buckley, Michigan. But perhaps more frequently, Norwegian Americans have retained their taste for Norwegian foods, such as those identified in appendix 5.

When the immigrants arrived from Norway, they came from a country with a state church, ostensibly Lutheran, and the majority identified with the Norwegian Lutheran churches in this country. Today this religious identity, when retained, is part of their cultural heritage and may be more important to them than religious doctrine, though changes in liturgy and hymnody have diluted whatever might remain of any Norwegian influence. In any case, most churches are no longer purely Norwegian, or Swedish, or even Scandinavian in character since being absorbed into the largest Lutheran body in the United States, known as the Evangelical Lutheran Church of America (ELCA). This has tended to weaken ethnic identification, which for a long time kept Norwegian Americans attached to their religious roots. The change has been part of a larger trend in America in which joining a different religious denomination is no longer considered unusual, as it surely was in those days when Norwegians who became Baptists, Methodists, Roman Catholics, Episcopalians, or Adventists were considered anomalies. Of course, there was always a segment of the immigrant population that never identified with any denomination and were secular, sometimes freethinking or otherwise simply indifferent to religion.

In recent years, there has been an explosion of interest in one's "roots," with many seeking help with genealogical research, at times complicated by the fact that in Norway, up to modern times, people did not always use surnames but instead were identified by patronymics, naming a person as the son of, for example, Ole—that is, as *Olson*. When surnames appeared, they were often place names, identifying the homestead or farm that the family worked or owned; these were often dispensed with when immigrating into the United States. Nevertheless, many have succeeded in tracing their families back through the nineteenth century into earlier times, and this has proved very rewarding. Sometimes the results can be quite surprising, as, for example, when the line of descent failed at some point to include an identifiable male ancestor in a particular generation—or when a princess from India is found lurking in the family tree.

While some Norwegian Americans have had relatives in Norway whom they could visit, perhaps the majority of those who have gone have done so as tourists. The lucky ones are those who could go to the communities where their grandparents or great-grandparents lived. There, they have been able to walk the lanes and streets where their forebears walked, and to sit in the pews in churches where they were baptized, confirmed, and married. On one occasion, a Norwegian American was taken up into the belfry of the parish church at Råde in Østfold, where he saw the bell that had rung at his grandmother's wedding more than a hundred years before. The bell was from the Danish period and hence must date from prior to 1814, the date of Norway's separation from Denmark. A frequent reaction in going to Norway among all but first-generation Norwegians, however, has been the lamenting of the loss of knowledge of the language.

The attitude toward one's ethnic identity among Norwegian Americans does not seem to translate into any particular stance toward their adopted

American identity. Some still consider themselves Norwegians first and Americans second, but these are surely very, very much in the minority. A cross section of political opinions may be found, though Norwegian Americans generally in earlier years identified more with the Republican party. Feelings toward non-Norwegians have certainly changed since the time when marriage with a Swede was considered a "mixed" marriage, and many were transformed during the Civil Rights struggle of the 1960s when, as Michigan Norwegian Americans, they came to understand how racial segregation was contrary to their egalitarian and democratic ideals. Most rejoiced, some even reported weeping with joy, at seeing Barack Obama inaugurated as the first African American President of the United States, even if they had failed to vote for him.

In Michigan, the main heritage organization in the state is the Sons of Norway, which now includes women as well as men. As a fraternal benefit society, its purpose is in part to preserve Norwegian culture by sponsoring classes, handicraft workshops, opportunities for travel, and language camps. It also provides numerous grants and scholarships, both at the national and the local levels. Free financial planning is offered, and Sons of Norway life insurance and annuities are available to members. Local lodges can offer further benefits for membership in addition to programs designed to illuminate Norwegian heritage at their monthly meetings.

The lodges active in Michigan are the following:

- Calumet: Ulseth Lodge
- Detroit: Nordkap Lodge
- Kalamazoo: Askaladen Lodge
- Lansing: Sonja Henie Lodge
- Muskegon: Sognefjord Lodge
- Pontiac: Samhold Lodge
- Suttons Bay: Christian Radich

For persons interested, these are easily reached through their websites, or through the website of the national organization (*www.sofn.com*), which maintains contact numbers for the officers.

Norwegian Hymns and Songs

The great bulk of Norwegian hymns in the *Lutheran Hymnary* of 1913 were settings by Ludvig Lindeman (1812–87), undoubtedly the most important figure in nineteenth-century Norwegian church music. Many of the examples represented in this hymnal are adaptations of folk hymns and songs based directly or indirectly on his work as a collector in the Norwegian countryside between 1850 and 1885. Sometimes, however, his music was adapted to extant English texts, as in the case of the well-known "Christ Whose Glory Fills the Skies," with words by Charles Wesley (no. 543), or the popular "For the Beauty of the Earth" (no. 529). His setting of the *Dies irae* ("Day of wrath! that day of mourning," no. 601) returns to the great thirteenth-century sequence attributed to Thomas of Celano, with its terrifying vision of the Last Day of history, when the time of grace will be past. Adapted from the Mass of the Dead, it would have been regarded as a remnant of Catholicism to be discarded by "low church" Lutherans, but is perfectly consistent with Luther's approval of praying for those who have passed through this life so long as the practice is not overdone.

As an admirer of J. S. Bach, Lindeman possessed a firm control of his musical material and deserves to be better known today for his work. He has not been given his due in the most recent Lutheran hymnals in America, though he also has a large presence in *Concordia*, the rival and widely used hymnal produced as an alternative to the *Hymnary*. Perhaps Lindeman's best-known hymn is the setting of N. F. S. Gruntvig's "Built on a Rock the church doth stand / Even when steeples are falling" (*Hymnary*, no 132), which retains its popularity today. There had been considerable resistance to Gruntvig, the great Danish clergyman and educator, among the Norwegian American clergy, but it would be hard to imagine the omission of this hymn.

Lindeman's influence can also be seen in "The Sun Has Gone Down" (*Hymnary*, no. 554), a Norwegian religious folksong. Included in the "Family Prayer" section of the *Hymnary*, it is a song of penitence the text of which, as translated by O. T. Sanden, is not untypical of Norwegian piety:

> *The sun has gone down,*
> *And peace has descended on country and town;*
> *The song-birds in silence flown to their nest,*
> *And flowers are closing their petals in rest;*
> *So closes my heart to annoyance and care,*
> *In homage and prayer,*
> *In homage and prayer.*[164]

Other Norwegian hymns in the *Hymnary* were taken from Zinck's *koralbog* (1801), Thomas Kingo's *Gradual* (1699), and other sources, but these were very few in number compared with Lindeman's contributions. The revised edition of the "low church" *Concordia* (1932) has a more generous selection of anonymous Norwegian folk tunes, such as "My Heart Is Longing to Praise My Savior" (no. 26), a setting of a Swedish text, the first five stanzas of which are given here on the following page.

On the other hand, the revised and enlarged *Concordia* of 1925 also included songs from the American Protestant repertoire, even two by Ira D. Sankey, the revivalist gospel songwriter. This collection additionally has a number of hymn settings by F. Melius Christiansen, the choral pioneer of St. Olaf College who had, as noted above, a major influence on American vocal music with his insistence on purity of tone, quite different from the vibrato-laden singing so prevalent in early twentieth-century America.

1. My heart is long-ing to praise my Sav-ior, And glo-ri-fy His
2. I walked in blind-ness; my soul was dy-ing; The prince of dark-ness
3. O bless-ed Je-sus, what Thou hast giv-en, Thru dy-ing on the
4. O Chris-tian friends, let our song as-cend-ing, Give hon-or, praise to
5. Soon we are home and shall stand be-fore Him; What mat-ter then, tho'

name in song and pray'r; For He has shown me His won-drous
held me in his pow'r. In pain I turned, to my Fa-ther
cross in bit-ter pain, Has filled my heart with the peace of
Him who set us free! Our trib-u-la-tions may seem un-
we have suf-fered here. Then He shall crown us, while we a-

fav-or And of-fered me all heav'n with Him to share.
cry-ing; He broke my chains and saved me in that hour.
heav-en; My win-ter's gone and spring is mine a-gain.
end-ing; But soon with Him we shall for-ev-er be.
dorn Him; So death and all our pains will dis-ap-pear.

"My Heart Is Longing to Praise My Savior"—from Concordia. *By permission of Augsburg-Fortress.*

A Norwegian American's Memory of the Occupation

Inger Thoen remembers that when there were air raids in Oslo during the war, she and her family would retreat to safety in the family basement. While there, her father would read to the children, their favorite children's book being *Snorre Sel* (*Snorre the Seal*),[165] which he gave to Inger and which, though "worn and falling apart," she keeps as a treasured possession. The story, she explains, "had a very special message." Her account of the story is as follows:

The book was about a beautiful little seal who lived far up in the north Atlantic with his mother. He was very vain and thought he had the most beautiful coat in the world. He spent hours and hours on the ice, looking at his own reflection and dreaming his life away. One day he got too far away from his mother and was lost. A pair of seagulls [Loop and Svang] with a false yellow glimmer in their eyes, and over their eyes red marks, were waiting for something, but the rest of the seagulls wanted nothing to do with them. He got into all kinds of dangers. He was flattered by a hungry polar bear [Brumlelabb] who wanted to eat him, and was almost swallowed by a great big killer whale [Glefs]. In the end he was rescued by a kind old walrus with a mustache [Uncle Bart], and returned to his mother.

Snorre the Seal and Brumlelabb, the killer whale. Illustration from Frithjof Sælen, Snorre Sel (1941).

The fable was explained by her as follows: "The little seal was Norway, the bad seagulls above were the Norwegian Nazis who betrayed him." These were identified in the fable by the colors yellow and red, designating Quisling and his followers. The threatening bear was Russia, and the killer whale was Germany. "The kind old walrus was England."

Not long following its publication, the Nazis discovered its "subversive" meaning and confiscated all the copies of the book they could find.

Appendix 5

Food

Those who have the impression that Scandinavian food is bland or uninteresting will be pleasantly surprised by a trip to Norway. It is true that the early Norwegians who came to Michigan of necessity had a very restricted diet, some of it less than palatable to the modern taste—for example, salt pork, which, though fried like bacon, was much less appealing. Spices were often restricted to salt and pepper, but potatoes served with melted butter and tasty potato rolls still will be a treat. But any good hotel in Norway will surprise one with an utterly luxurious display of pickled herring, stuffed eggs, pancakes with lingonberries, sausages, toast and preserves, sometimes cheeses, and more, along with, of course, properly brewed coffee such as one never finds at an American motel that pretends to serve a "continental breakfast." And for an afternoon snack, nothing could be more delicious, along with, again, good Norwegian coffee.

Some Norwegian foods still may be purchased in supermarkets or specialty delicatessens. These include flatbread, herring, cheeses such as *gjetost* (goat cheese) and *primost* (whey cheese), and other good things. Meatloaf, meatballs, and creamed green peas are part of the American diet, albeit made with differing ingredients.

The sample recipes included here are ones from Michigan kitchens, mainly from contributions from Sons of Norway members. They can of course be adapted to one's taste. Many of these are only made at Christmas, but are regarded as prized heritage food. Organic ingredients are recommended, though it will be recognized that availability must dictate in this regard. Naturally, transfats should be avoided, as should aluminum cookware. Special equipment is required for some recipes, as specified.

Stuffed Eggs

4 hard-boiled eggs
2 Tbsp. of chopped smoked salmon, ham, or anchovy fillets
1 tsp. butter
2½ Tbsp. of cheese, grated (cheddar recommended)

Peel eggs carefully, then cut in halves lengthwise. Remove yolks and mix with other ingredients, then stuff the egg whites with this.

Fruktsuppe (Fruit Soup)

½ lb. dried prunes
½ lb. mixed fruit, dried
1 cup sugar
1 stick cinnamon
½ cup pearl tapioca
1 cup grape juice
Juice of 1 lemon

Soak prunes and dried fruit in 2 quarts water for 3 hours. Then bring to boil, and add sugar and cinnamon. Cook slowly until fruit is tender. Remove fruit and bring juice to boil, then thicken with tapioca. Remove from stove and add lemon juice and grape juice. May also be made with apples, raisins, peaches, blueberries, or cherries.

Rømmegrøt

1½ cup sour cream (high fat, natural, no additives)
1½ cups whole milk
1½ cups flour

Cover and simmer sour cream for approximately 15 minutes; sift in a third of the flour. Simmer, then skim off butterfat and save. Sift in the remainder of the flour, thin with milk that has been brought to boil, then add remaining flour and bring to boil. Stir with whisk until the desired smoothness is reached. Simmer for 12 minutes. Add fat, salt, sugar, and cinnamon to taste.

Norwegian Meatballs

2 lbs. ground beef

2 eggs

1 cup milk

½ cup flour (finely crumbled dry bread may substitute)

½ tsp. pepper

½ tsp. salt

1 finely ground onion

Blend all ingredients, form into meatballs by hand. In frying pan, pour 2 tablespoons of cooking oil and bring heat to medium. Add meatballs, gently turn when cooking until brown. May also be baked on a baking pan for 10–15 minutes. Serve with potatoes or cooked rice.

Sylte (Headcheese)

5 lbs. pork shoulder (very lean)

1 pork hock

1 cup water

salt and pepper

2 tsp. allspice

½ cup grated onion

Cook ingredients until *very* tender, then cool. Cut into pieces. Use small amount of fat, but not all of it. If necessary, dissolve 1 package of unflavored gelatin in a small amount of water to add to meat mixture and liquid from cooking pan. Add allspice, onion, salt, and pepper to taste. Mold using a bread pan or similar container, and pour mixture into it. Liquid should come up to the top of the meat mixture in mold. To serve, slice thinly.

Potato Lefse

5 cups riced potatoes
1 tsp. salt
2 Tbsp. butter or thick sweet cream (whipping cream)
2 cups flour

Mix well and shape into balls large enough to be rolled like piecrust to the size of an average dinner plate. Keep balls in a covered bowl in refrigerator until ready to roll. Use a pastry cloth and sleeved rolling pin so as to use as little extra flour as possible. Bake on an ungreased pancake griddle or an electric lefse baker. Bake one side until golden brown spots appear, then turn and bake other side. Finished lefse should be moist and pliable. Stack circles on tea towels as they are baked and keep covered with towel to prevent drying. When all are baked, place towel and all into a plastic bag and refrigerate until used—if all are not eaten warm.

To serve, butter each on one side (sugar may be added), fold in half, then in quarters, and roll so sugar will not spill and fold into a handy size for holding and eating.—*(Houghton, MI) Daily Mining Gazette*

Krumkake

1 cup sugar
½ cup butter
3 eggs
½ tsp. salt (optional)
½ cup sweet cream
1½ cups milk
1 tsp. vanilla extract
Flour

Mix sugar and butter to a creamy consistency, then add eggs, cream, and milk in that order. Add flour until a soft dough is attained. Place a portion (a rounded teaspoon) on hot krumkake iron and bake until brown. Roll into cone shape immediately, preferably on a wooden krumkake cone.

Kringle

2 cups sugar
1 stick of margarine or butter (preferred)
1 egg
½ tsp. salt
1 tsp. soda in sour cream
1 tsp. baking powder
5½ cups flour
1 cup sour cream
1 cup buttermilk
1 tsp. anise seed

Prepare evening before baking, keep chilled. Mix melted butter or margarine and sugar, add cream and buttermilk, then add egg and anise seed gradually. Add dry materials to the creamed mixture and mix by hand, using a knife or spoon. Using small portions at a time, roll dough by hand to 8–10 inches, cut off a piece and roll until 5–6 inches (finger thickness). Shake into a double twist (around twice and cross, pick up and place on top of center). Then pick this up and slightly stretch on baking sheet (six per sheet). Bake at 425° for around 10 to 12 minutes or until browned.

Fattigmann

4 egg yolks
2 egg whites
4 Tbsp. sugar
4 Tbsp. sweet cream
1½ cups flour
2 shot glasses of brandy (optional)
½ tsp. ground cardamom

Whip eggs, sugar, and cream together, stir in flour, and mix until dough is smooth. Let stand for a few hours. Roll out fairly thin (½-inch thickness). Cut into diamond shape, cut slit in middle and pull a corner through to make a bow. Deep fry in vegetable oil. Before serving, sprinkle with powdered sugar.

Rosettes

1 cup flour
1 egg
1 cup milk
1 tsp. sugar
vegetable oil for deep frying

Mix batter until smooth and of the consistency of thick cream (no lumps). Prepare vegetable oil for deep frying by bringing to approximately 370°. Insert rosette iron into the oil, then dip into the batter; fry until golden brown in color. Remove and place on brown paper to drain. May be sprinkled with powered sugar.

Sandbakkels

1 cup vegetable shortening or butter (preferred)
1½ cups sugar
1 egg
½ tsp. salt (optional)
2 cups flour (sifted)
1 tsp. almond extract

Mix butter or vegetable shortening, sugar, and egg until combined; then add almond extract. Press dough into sandbakkel tart molds and bake in 350° oven until slightly brown around edges. Cool slightly and remove from molds. The molds must be greased for first-time use, and thereafter do not wash with soap and water. Wipe out and store in freezer.

Sprutbakkels (Spritz)

½ cup butter
½ cup vegetable shortening
1 cup sugar
1 egg
½ tsp. vanilla extract

½ tsp. almond extract
½ tsp. salt
3 cups flour

Mix butter, shortening, and sugar. Add egg and beat well, then add vanilla and almond extract, and flour. Use cookie press, and place on baking sheet; bake at 350°. Observe until beginning to become tan at edges.

Norwegian Coffee

Add 2 eggs, including shells, to 1 pint freshly ground coffee, add a little water to moisten. Add 1 gallon of boiling water, cook for 3 minutes. Remove from heat and allow to set for 10 minutes. Drain coffee from grounds. Makes large quantity. For making less, retain proportions as much as possible.

Notes

1. Carlton C. Qualey, *Norwegian Settlement in the United States* (1938; reprint, New York: Arno Press, 1970), 176–77; Kendric Charles Babcock, *The Scandinavian Element in the United States* (Urbana: University of Illinois, 1914), 212, 214; Jack Glazier and Arthur W. Helweg, *Ethnicity in Michigan* (East Lansing: Michigan State University Press, 2001), 82.

2. See, for example, Angelo Forte, Richard Oram, and Frederick Pedersen, *Viking Empires* (Cambridge: Cambridge University Press, 2005).

3. Information communicated by Sheila White.

4. Quoted by Albert O. Barton, "Norwegian-American Emigration Societies of the Forties and Fifties," *Norwegian-American Studies* 3 (1928): 23–42.

5. Ibid.

6. Ingrid Semmingsen, *Norway to America: A History of the Migration*, trans. Einar Haugen (Minneapolis: University of Minnesota Press, 1978), 99.

7. Barke (Birkeland) Family Records, Norwegian-American Historical Association, Northfield, MN, P.1427.

8. Letter of July 26, 1846, Norwegian-American Historical Association, P.314.

9. See O. E. Rølvaag, *Concerning Our Heritage*, trans. Solveig Zempel (Northfield, MN: Norwegian-American Historical Association, 1998).

10. Ibid., 22.

11. Alma A. Gutterson and Regina Hilleboe Christensen, eds., *Norse-American* **139**

Women (St. Paul: Lutheran Free Church Publishing Company, 1926), 107.

12. Martin Ulvestad, *Nordmændene i Amerika, deres Historie og Rekord* (Minneapolis: History Book Company's Forlag, 1907), 192.

13. O. E. Rølvaag, *Giants in the Earth*, trans. Lincoln Colcord and the author (New York: Harper and Brothers, 1927), 45–46. After 1854, immigrants could also take the Canadian railroad to Detroit; see Semmingsen, *Norway to America*, 62.

14. Johan Gasmann, "From New York to Wisconsin in 1844," trans. Carleton C. Qualey, *Norwegian-American Studies* 5 (1930): 30–49.

15. Norwegian-American Historical Association, P.1427. The location of Stony Creek is uncertain, but it was in the western part of the state. When Stubhaug first came to this location, he saw what he thought was lush grass—which, however, turned out to be leeks.

16. George W. Hilton, *Lake Michigan Passenger Steamers* (Stanford, CA: Stanford University Press, 2002), 49, 279–93.

17. Semmingsen, *Norway to America*, 124.

18. Knut Gjerset, *Norwegian Sailors on the Great Lakes* (Northfield, MN: Norwegian-American Historical Association, 1928), 54. This work is an invaluable reference source.

19. Ibid., 56, 133, 167.

20. Ibid., 164–65.

21. Ibid., 71.

22. Ibid., 190.

23. Ibid., 166.

24. Ibid., 49, 117.

25. Arthur C. and Lucy F. Frederickson, *History of the Ann Arbor Auto and Train Ferries* (Frankfort, MI: Gull's Nest Publishing, 1994), 101.

26. Ibid., 102, 105.

27. Gjerset, *Norwegian Sailors*, 188.

28. Howard Sivertson, *Once upon an Isle: The Story of Fishing Families on Isle Royale* (Mt. Horeb, WI: Mt. Horeb Folk Museum, 1992), 1; Dorothy Simonson, *The Diary of an Isle Royale School Teacher* (Houghton, MI: Isle Royale Natural History Association, 1988), passim.

29. Photograph in Sivertson, *Once upon an Isle*, 19.

30. Ibid., 34–35; Elling Seglem, *Diaries of an Isle Royale Fisherman*, ed. Robert Root and Jill Burkland (Houghton, MI: Isle Royale Natural History Association, 2002), 11.

31. Sivertson, *Once upon an Isle*, 46.

32. Ibid., 44–46.

33. Simonson, *The Diary*, 129 and passim; see also Seglem, *Diaries*, 127.

34. Sivertson, *Once upon an Isle*, 13.

35. Ibid., 58.

36. Seglem, *Diaries*, 126–27.

37. Simonson, *The Diary*, 99.

38. Sivertson, *Once upon an Isle*, 45.

39. Peter Peterson Family Records, Norwegian-American Historical Association, P.881.

40. Both harvesting with a scythe and with a primitive early reaper are illustrated in Odd S. Lovoll, *The Promise of America: A History of the Norwegian-American People* (Minneapolis: University of Minnesota Press, 1984), 37–38.

41. See the detailed examination, which is also applicable to Michigan, by Reidar Bakken, "Acculturation and Farmsteads in Coon Valley, Wisconsin, from 1850 to 1930," in Marion John Nelson, ed., *Material Culture and People's Art among the Norwegians in America* (Northfield, MN: Norwegian-American Historical Association, 1994), 73–91.

42. Marion J. Nelson, "The Material Culture and Folk Arts of the Norwegians in America," in *Perspectives on American Folk Art*, ed. Ian M. G. Quimby and Scott T. Swank (New York: W. W. Norton, 1980), 82–86.

43. "Melkild Family History," personal typescript, courtesy of the late Martin A. Melkild and Elizabeth Melkild, Traverse City, MI, 1–2.

44. Ibid., 5.

45. Ibid., 7–9.

46. Jean Kreger Darling, *Bavers in America, 1888–1988* (privately published, 1998), 5–9; and information communicated by members of the Baver family, especially Pauline Baver (b. 1915), who still lives on the family farm.

47. Wagbo Family History, Norwegian-American Historical Association, P.1183.

48. Alice Prescott Kyes, *Romance of Muskegon* (1937; reprint, Muskegon, MI: Muskegon Public Schools, 1971), 89.

49. William Gerald Rector, *Log Transportation in the Lakes Lumber Industry, 1840–1918* (Glendale, CA: Arthur H. Clark, 1953), 195ff.

50. *Life in a Lumber Camp: A Series of Articles Published in the Alpena News in 1914* (Alpena, MI: Alpena News and Montmorency County Tribune, 1990).

51. See the illustration in Jeremy W. Kilar, *Michigan's Lumber Towns: Lumbermen*

and Laborers in Saginaw, Bay City, and Muskegon, 1870–1905 (Detroit: Wayne State University Press, 1990), 251.

52. The engines were not attached to the saws by a direct drive shaft, but rather a power belt was used—another source of danger for the workers. A photo of a Corliss steam engine appears in Allen B. Blacklock, *History of Elberta* (Manistee, MI: West Graf, 1975), 32.

53. Ibid., 26, 31.

54. See ibid., pl. following 163, and for commentary, 167.

55. John Fitzmaurice, *Shanty Boy: The Shanty Boy, or Life in a Lumber Camp* (1889; reprint, Historical Society of Michigan, 1978), 175, as quoted in Kilar, *Michigan's Lumber Towns*, 73, and see ibid., 190, for photograph showing prostitutes.

56. Kilar, *Michigan's Lumber Towns*, 74.

57. Kyes, *Romance of Muskegon*, 125.

58. Ulvestad, *Nordmændene i Amerika*, 192.

59. Kilar, *Michigan's Lumber Towns*, 182.

60. Kyes, *Romance of Muskegon*, 94.

61. For a photograph showing the devastation resulting from clear-cutting, see Kay Hommel et al., *Shared Moments: A Journey through Time* (Benzonia: Benzie Area Historical Society, 2007), 27.

62. Qualey, *Norwegian Settlement in the United States*, 183–84.

63. The average age at death for those born abroad was thirty-five, for those born in America even lower; see Larry Lankton, *Cradle to Grave: Life, Work, and Death at the Lake Superior Copper Mines* (New York: Oxford University Press, 1991), 112.

64. *Copper Country Journal: The Diary of Schoolmaster Henry Hobart, 1863–1864*, ed. Philip P. Mason (Detroit: Wayne State University Press, 1991), 205–7 and passim.

65. David J. Krause, *The Making of the Mining District: Keweenaw Native Copper, 1500–1870* (Detroit: Wayne State University Press, 1992), 244.

66. Arthur W. Thurner, *Strangers and Sojourners: A History of Michigan's Keweenaw Peninsula* (Detroit: Wayne State University Press, 1994), 192–95.

67. "1913 Massacre" by Woody Guthrie, *Struggle* (1946), copyright New York: Sanga Music, downloaded from *http://www.geocities.com/Nashville/3448/1913.html*.

68. Blegen, *Norwegian Migration to America*, 415–16.

69. Ibid., 416–17.

70. Paul W. Robson, *Calumet and Hecla: Pioneer, Producer and Pacemaker* (New York: Newcomen Society, 1966), 11.

71. Krause, *The Making of the Mining District*, 243.

72. Quoted in the *Newsletter of the Norwegian Lutheran Church Historical Society of Calumet*, 5, no. 1 (August 2007): 2.

73. Qualey, *Norwegian Settlement in the United States*, 185.

74. George Newett, "History of Ishpeming Ski Club," in Harold A. Grinden, ed., *History of the National Ski Association and the Ski Sport in the United States of America, 1840 to 1931* (Duluth, MN: National Ski Association, n.d.), 14.

75. See especially E. John B. Allen, *The Culture and Sport of Skiing from Antiquity to World War II* (Amherst: University of Massachusetts Press, 2007), 24–30; and Frida Warra, "U.S. National Ski Hall of Fame: Origins in Ishpeming, Michigan," in E. John B. Allen, ed., *2002 International Ski History Congress: Selected Papers* (New Hartford, CT: International Ski History Association, 2002), 296ff.

76. In addition to the works cited above, see also E. John B. Allen, "The Modernization of Skisport: Ishpeming's Contribution to American Skiing," *Michigan Historical Review* 16 (1990): 1–20.

77. For a photograph of the Norden Club established in 1887, see E. John B. Allen, *From Skisport to Skiing: One Hundred Years of an American Sport, 1840–1940* (Amherst: University of Massachusetts Press, 1993), 51.

78. See Grinden, ed., *History of the National Ski Association*.

79. Ibid., 15; Allen, *From Skisport to Skiing*, 66.

80. The years when these engineers arrived had seen the rise of freethinking, which challenged the conventional religion of Norway. The best-known exponent was the dramatist Henrik Ibsen, but it had penetrated deeply into the thinking of those who worked in the scientific and technical fields.

81. Kenneth Bjork, *Saga in Steel and Concrete* (Northfield, MN: Norwegian-American Historical Association, 1947), 36–37; and for immigration statistics, see ibid., 24–28.

82. Quoted in translation by Carleton C. Qualey, "Pioneer Scandinavian Settlement in Michigan," *Michigan History* 24 (1940): 437.

83. Bjork, *Saga in Steel and Concrete*, 160–61, pl. facing 133.

84. Ibid., 167.

85. Bjork, *Saga in Steel and Concrete*, 167–68.

86. Patricia Zacharias, "The Building of the Detroit-Windsor Tunnel," *Detroit News*, January 25, 2000, *http://apps.detnews.com/apps/history/index.php?id=51*, accessed November 27, 2008; Bjork, *Saga in Steel and Concrete*, 171–82.

87. Bjork, *Saga in Steel and Concrete*, 197–201.

88. Drawing by Dennis Darling, after engineering diagram, as reproduced in Zacha-

rias, "The Building of the Detroit-Windsor Tunnel."

89. Zacharias, "The Building of the Detroit-Windsor Tunnel."

90. Bjork, *Saga in Steel and Concrete*, 389.

91. Ibid., 390.

92. N. F. S. Hanson Papers, Norwegian-American Historical Association, P.572.

93. Daniel Nelson, *Farm and Factory: Workers in the Midwest* (Bloomington: Indiana University Press, 1995), 79.

94. Quoted by Bjork, *Saga in Steel and Concrete*, 390.

95. See Florence M. Manning, "Carl G. Barth, 1860–1939: A Sketch," *Norwegian-American Studies and Records* 13 (1943): 114–32.

96. Ralph Helgeby Papers, Bentley Historical Library, University of Michigan, 7188.

97. Information conveyed in responses to survey submitted to Michigan Sons of Norway lodge members.

98. C. Lawrence Lind, "Upper Peninsula Girl is Winning Honors in the Musical World," *Cloverland* (August 1919): 18, included on Braastad website: *http://www .richardb.us/Braastad/Borghild.html*, accessed December 7, 2008.

99. "A Family History of the Olsen Family Which Came to Western Michigan from Norway in 1867," Bentley Historical Library, University of Michigan.

100. Arthur W. Thurner, *Strangers and Sojourners: A History of Michigan's Keweenaw Peninsula* (Detroit: Wayne State University Press, 1994), 132–33.

101. See "Mack Trucks' Peterson," *Fortune* 53, no. 1 (January 1956): 100–101.

102. *(Frankfort, MI) Record Patriot*, June 25, 2008, 1, 3.

103. Information kindly provided by Laurie Sommers.

104. Lawrence M. Sommers, ed., *Atlas of Michigan* (East Lansing: Michigan State University Press, 1977), 1–2.

105. Norwegian-American Historical Association, MSS. 1125.

106. Ulvestad, *Nordmændene i Amerika*, 192; and information supplied by the Rev. William Uetricht.

107. E. Clifford Nelson, *The Lutheran Church among Norwegian Americans*, 2 vols. (Minneapolis: Augsburg, 1960), 1:3–12; and see also the valuable perspective of L. DeAne Lagerquist, *In America the Men Milk the Cows: Factors of Gender, Ethnicity, and Religion in the Americanization of Norwegian-American Women* (Brooklyn, NY: Carlson, 1991), esp. 13–32.

108. Some of these issues were addressed by the late Hans Jørgen Holman in a paper read at a Western Michigan University Medieval Institute Round Table in September 1982 and subsequently published in revised form as "Centonization

Technique in the Vocal Folk Music of Norway," *Michigan Academician* 15 (1983): 333–45.

109. See Gracia Grindal, "Dano-Norwegian Hymnody in America," *Lutheran Quarterly*, n.s. 6 (1992): 257–58.

110. An instrument used by the *klokker* called the *psalmodikon*, a type of monochord, was played with a bow, but this was for working out the music of hymns at home in preparation for services; ibid., 263–64.

111. One Scandinavian tradition had it that the technique of folk fiddling was initially taught by trolls.

112. See, for example, J. C. K. Preus, "Norwegian State Church to American Free Church," *Norwegian-American Studies* 25 (1972): 186–224.

113. Nelson, *The Lutheran Church among Norwegian Americans*, 1:13–23.

114. The connection with healthful vegetarian foods will be clarified by noting that Adventists had a role in founding the Kellogg and Post cereal companies in Battle Creek, where there was also as early as 1873 a well-respected "Sanitorium" or hospital.

115. Theodore C. Blegen, *Norwegian Migration to America* (1940; reprint, Haskell House, 1969), 101–74; Nelson, *The Lutheran Church among Norwegian Americans*, passim.

116. The Formula of Concord was the basis of the most rigid Lutheran orthodoxy and hence was found widely unpalatable among Norwegians and Norwegian-Americans. This document ushered in a severe period of orthodoxy in the Lutheran churches of Europe throughout much of the seventeenth century, until the rise of Pietism. The latter movement is particularly associated with the name of Phillip Spener, and while not being favorable to classical church music such as J. S. Bach's, it fostered many of the congregational hymns in the Norwegian and Norwegian-American repertoire.

117. Lovoll, *The Promise of America*, 208.

118. The only church in America to have retained the native language on a regular basis is the Norwegian Memorial Church in Minneapolis.

119. O. E. Rølvaag, *Their Fathers' God*, trans. Trygve M. Ager (New York: Harper and Brothers, 1931), 207 (emphasis in original).

120. See the extended survey in Grindal, "Dano-Norwegian Hymnody," 257–316.

121. For additional commentary, see appendix 3.

122. See *Norsk Salme Bok* (Verbum, 1985), no. 245; an alternate version from Heddal appears as no. 244.

123. Valuable information that is also relevant to Michigan is contained in Larson's University of Minnesota dissertation, "Scandinavian-American Folk Dance Music of the Norwegians in Minnesota," 2 vols. (1975).

124. Nils Grinde, *A History of Norwegian Music*, trans. William H. Halverson and Leland B. Sateren (Lincoln: University of Nebraska Press, 1991), 87–91.

125. See LeRoy Larson, "The Aakhus Concert Company: Norwegian-American Entertainers," in *Sacra/Profana: Studies in Sacred and Secular Music for Johannes Riedel*, ed. Audrey Ekdahl Davidson and Clifford Davidson (Minneapolis: Friends of Minnesota Music, 1985), 114–18.

126. See Hardanger Fiddle Association of America website: *http://www.hfaa.org*, accessed January 15, 2009.

127. Personal communication.

128. This point was made by Larry Syndergaard, a ballad specialist, in conversation.

129. See Holman, "Centonization Technique in the Vocal Folk Music of Norway," 335.

130. See, for example, the survey by Gunnar Bugge, *Stave-Churches in Norway* (Dreyers Forlag, 1983).

131. Marion Nelson, ed., *Norwegian Folk Art: The Migration of a Tradition* (New York: Abbeville Press, 1995), 61–64.

132. Darrell D. Henning, Marion J. Nelson, and Roger L. Welsch, *Norwegian-American Wood Carving of the Upper Midwest* (Decorah, IA: Vesterheim, 1978), 83–84, figs. 68–69.

133. See especially Kristin M. Anderson, "Altars in the Norwegian-American Church: An Opportunity for Folk Expression," in *Material Culture and People's Art among the Norwegians in America*, ed. Marion John Nelson (Northfield, MN: Norwegian-American Historical Association, 1994), 199–226.

134. For a survey of Norwegian American dress and its adaption to American styles, see Carol Colburn, "'Well, I Wondered When I Saw You, What All Those New Clothes Meant': Interpreting the Dress of Norwegian-American Immigrants," in Nelson, ed., *Material Culture and People's Art*, 118–55.

135. Ibid., 144–46.

136. Aagot Noss, "Rural Norwegian Dress and Its Symbolic Function," and Carol Huset Colburn, "Norwegian Folk Dress in America," in Nelson, ed., *Norwegian Folk Art*, 149–55, figs. 7, 23–24, and 157–69.

137. Guttersen and Christiansen, eds., *Norse-American Women*, 192.

138. See Anderson, "Altars in the Norwegian-American Church," 206.

139. Nils Ellingsgard, "Rosemaling: A Folk Art in Migration," in Nelson, ed., *Norwegian Folk Art*, 190–94, and catalogue items 146–205.

140. Best known is her *Traditional Norwegian Rosemaling* (1970), which is reported to have sold 37,000 copies.

141. Thomas Keightley, *The Fairy Mythology* (London, 1880), 116–17. For the similar folktale featuring St. Olaf, see Reidar T. Christiansen, *Folktales of Norway*, trans. Pat Shaw Iversen (Chicago: University of Chicago Press, 1964), 5–6; here the reward was to be St. Olaf's head.

142. Ibid., xxix.

143. For a recipe for *grøt*, see appendix 5.

144. The folklorist Katharine M. Briggs noted at a conference that a variant of this tale had been recorded in Yorkshire, a sign perhaps of its antiquity since it may have been imported in the days when York was still a Norse kingdom.

145. Larson, "Scandinavian Folk Dance Music," 1:29–30.

146. Eivind D. Aakhus, *Minne Frå Norge og Amerika* (Kristiansund: Johanssen & Tangens, 1932), 58–60, as cited in Larson, "Scandinavian Folk Dance Music," 42.

147. Kathleen Stokker, *Folklore Fights the Nazis: Humor in Occupied Norway, 1940–1945* (Madison, NJ: Fairleigh Dickinson University Press, 1995), 123.

148. Inger Thoen, "Memories of the Occupation during WW II as Seen through the Eyes of a Child," in *Remembrances of World War II in Norway* ([Indianapolis]: Fifth District Sons of Norway, 1998), 39.

149. Ibid., 41.

150. A. N. Rygg, *American Relief for Norway* (Chicago: Arnsen Press, 1947), 28.

151. Their mother's letters, in translation, and commentary appear in Catherine Hoff Mount and Karen Hoff Lafnear, *Six Years to Sunrise*, ed. Harry Knitter (Clarkston, MI: Kordene Publications, 2000).

152. Ibid., 159, 163.

153. Letter to Ralph Helgeby, in Helgeby Papers, Bentley Historical Library, University of Michigan, 7188.

154. Thoen, "Memories of the Occupation," 40–41.

155. Letter from Leif Melsom to Ralph Helgeby, Helgeby Papers.

156. Mount and Lafnear, *Six Years to Sunrise*, 153.

157. See Catherine Groth Sparrow, "Little Norway–Muskoka–Vesle Skaugum: Training Centers of the Royal Norwegian Air Force in Canada," *American Scandinavian Review* 30 (1942): 203–15.

158. Rygg, *American Relief*, 251–52.

159. Helgeby Papers.

160. Rygg, *American Relief*, 76–86.

161. Snorre Sturlason, *Heimskringla: The Norse King Sagas*, trans. S. Lang, revised ed. (London: J. M. Dent and Sons, 1951), 93.

162. The term was coined by the Norwegian American economist Thorstein Veblen, whose *Theory of the Leisure Class* (1899) is a classic and a sharp challenge to modern consumerism.

163. Kathleen Stokker, *Keeping Christmas: Yuletide Traditions in Norway and the New Land* (St. Paul: Minnesota Historical Society, 2000), 110–14. While this work is the best, there are numerous short but useful accounts of Norwegian Christmas customs in popular books and articles that are quite easily accessible. For examples, see Bent Vanberg, *Of Norwegian Ways* (Minneapolis: Dillon Press, 1970), 80–85, or various December issues of *Viking*, the magazine of the Sons of Norway.

164. In the *Hymnary*, two stanzas follow, ending with the words "My errors and failings I deeply regret, / forgive and forget!" *Concordia* gives a fourth stanza, committing "body and soul" to God's care.

165. Frithjof Sælen, *Snorre Sel* (Bergen: John Griegs Forlag, 1941).

For Further Reference

Allen, E. John B. *The Culture and Sport of Skiing from Antiquity to World War II*. Amherst: University of Massachusetts Press, 2007.

Babcock, Kendric Charles. *The Scandinavian Element in the United States*. 1914; reprint, New York: Arno Press, 1969.

Bjork, Kenneth. *Saga in Steel and Concrete*. Northfield, MN: Norwegian-American Historical Association, 1947.

Blegen, Theodore C. *Norwegian Migration to America: The American Transition*. 1940; reprint, New York: Haskell House, 1969.

———, ed. *Land of Their Choice: The Immigrants Write Home*. Minneapolis: University of Minnesota Press, 1955.

Christiansen, Reidar T. *Folktales of Norway*. Translated by Pat Shaw Iversen. Chicago: University of Chicago Press, 1964.

Ekstrand, Florence. *The Best of the Old Church Cookbooks*. Seattle: Welcome Press, 1988.

Forte, Angelo, Richard Oram, and Frederik Pedersen. *Viking Empires*. Cambridge: Cambridge University Press, 2005.

Gjerset, Knut. *Norwegian Sailors on the Great Lakes*. Northfield, MN: Norwegian-American Historical Association, 1928.

Glazier, Jack, and Arthur W. Helweg. *Ethnicity in Michigan*. East Lansing: Michigan State University Press, 2001.

Grindal, Gracia. "Dano-Norwegian Hymnody in America." *Lutheran Quarterly*, n.s. 6 (1992): 257–315.

Grinde, Nils. *A History of Norwegian Music*. Translated by William H. Halverson and Leland B. Sateren. Lincoln: University of Nebraska Press, 1991.

Hamsun, Knut. *The Cultural Life of Modern America*. Translated by Barbara Gordon Morgridge. Cambridge, MA: Harvard University Press, 1969.

Hancks, Jeffrey W. *Scandinavians in Michigan*. East Lansing: Michigan State University Press, 2006.

Hilton, George W. *The Great Lakes Car Ferries*. Berkeley, CA: Howell-North, 1962.

———. *Lake Michigan Passenger Steamers*. Stanford, CA: Stanford University Press, 2002.

Kilar, Jeremy W. *Michigan's Lumber Towns: Lumbermen and Laborers in Saginaw, Bay City, and Muskegon, 1870–1905*. Detroit: Wayne State University Press, 1990.

Krause, David J. *The Making of a Mining District: Keweenaw Native Copper, 1500–1870*. Detroit: Wayne State University Press, 1992.

Lagerquist, L. DeAne. *In America Men Milk the Cows: Factors of Gender, Ethnicity, and Religion in the Americanization of Norwegian-American Women*. Brooklyn, NY: Carlson, 1991.

Lovoll, Odd S. *The Promise of America: A History of the Norwegian-American People*. Minneapolis: University of Minnesota Press, 1984.

MacGregor, Sheila. *Traditional Scandinavian Knitting*. Mineola, NY: Dover, 1984.

Miller, Margaret M., and Sigmund Aarseth. *Norwegian Rosemaling: Decorative Painting on Wood*. New York: Charles Scribner's Sons, 1974.

Nelson, E. Clifford. *The Lutheran Church among Norwegian-Americans*. 2 vols. Minneapolis: Augsburg, 1960.

Nelson, Marion John, ed. *Material Culture and People's Art among the Norwegians in America*. Northfield, MN: Norwegian-American Historical Association, 1994.

———, ed. *Norwegian Folk Art: The Migration of a Tradition*. New York: Abbeville Press, 1995.

Qualey, Carleton C. *Norwegian Settlement in the United States*. 1938; reprint, New York: Arno Press, 1970.

Rølvaag, O. E. *Concerning Our Heritage*. Translated by Solveig Zempel. Northfield, MN: Norwegian-American Historical Association, 1998.

Semmingsen, Ingrid. *Norway to America: A History of the Migration*. Translated by Einar Haugen. Minneapolis: University of Minnesota Press, 1978.

Sivertson, Howard. *Once upon an Isle: The Story of Fishing Families on Isle Royale*. Mount Horeb, WI: Wisconsin Folk Museum, 1992.

Sommers, Lawrence M., ed. *Atlas of Michigan*. East Lansing: Michigan State University Press, 1977.

Sons of Norway Songbook. Minneapolis: Supreme Lodge of the Sons of Norway, 1948.

Stokker, Kathleen. *Keeping Christmas: Yuletide Traditions in Norway and the New Land*. St. Paul: Minnesota Historical Society, 2000.

Thurner, Arthur W. *Strangers and Sojourners: A History of Michigan's Keweenaw Peninsula*. Detroit: Wayne State University Press, 1994.

Vanberg, Bent. *Of Norwegian Ways*. Minneapolis: Dillon Press, 1970.

Index

A

Aakhus, Daniel and Gecina, 80–81, 98

America (steamer), 23

American Relief for Norway, 105–107

Anderson, Abraham, 18

Andsnes, Leif Ove, 84

Ann Arbor: University of Michigan at, 63

Ann Arbor No. 4 (car ferry), 20–21

Asgaard, Haagen, 48

Askeladden (Ash Lad), 96–98

Atlas of Michigan, 61

Auburn Heights, MI, 104

Auensen, Peter, 79

B

Barke, Charles, 9–10

Barth, Carl G., 55–56

Battle Creek, MI, 15, 145 (n. 114)

Baver, Ellen, 63–64

Baver, Sivert, 34, 39

Baver family: farmstead, 28–29; Peder
  and Marit, 33–34

Bay City, MI, 38–39, 52

"Behold a host arrayed in white," 72–73

Bergen, Norway, 96, 104; University of,
  61

Bergh, Hans J., 67

Berrien Springs, MI: Andrews University
  at, 70, 84

Birkeland, Karl. *See* Barke, Charles

Bjornson, Bjornsterne, 83

Boat of Longing, 71

Braastad, Borghild, 58

Braastad, Frederick, 57–58, 118

Bridal march, or procession, 81, 83

Buffalo, NY: transit through, 13

"Built on a Rock" (hymn by N. F. S.
  Gruntvig), 126

bunader (Norwegian costume), 82,
87–89

Dreutzer, O. E., 42

Duluth, MN, 23–24, 50, 63

C

Calumet, MI, 42–45, 57, 67; Lutheran
church at, 43–45, 86, 92; Norwegian
Lutheran Church Historical Society
at, 43

Calumet and Hecla Mining Co., 43, 58

Centennial Mine, 58

Charlevoix, MI, 18

Chicago, IL, 14–15, 17, 32, 37, 51–52

Chippewa Harbor, MI, 24

Christiansen, F. Melius, 72, 126

churches: Lutheran, 35, 39, 43–45, 67–77,
86, 92, 106, 117–19, 121–22; other, 39,
70, 77, 106, 117, 119, 122, 145 (n. 114)

City of Grand Haven (schooner), 18–19

clear cutting: deleterious effects of, 40

Cletus Schneider (steamer), 21–22

Cliff Mine (copper mine at Clifton, MI),
41–42

Clover (lighthouse tender), 18

Code, Karin Løberg and David, 81

Concordia, 73, 125–26

confirmation class, 87

D

Dawn (sailing ship), 17

Dearborn, MI, 54

Detroit, MI, 13–14, 37, 51–53, 106; automobile tunnel at, 52–53; bridge to
Belle Isle, 52; railroad tunnel at, 52

diet, 24, 35, 37–38, 108–110, 131, 137–38,
145 (n. 114)

D. O. Mills (steamship), 19

E

East Jordan, MI, 34–35

economy: Norwegian, changes in, 8

Ede, David, 60

Eirik Bloodaxe (king of York), 6

Eirikson, Leif, 1

Elberta, MI, 63–65: farmstead at, 28–29,
33, 39

Emstad, Marit, 90

England, 5–6, 77

Erdahl, Ingolf, 52

Erikson, Theresa, 11

Evangeliets Sendebud (Adventist newspaper), 119

F

Fairies. *See* nisser

Faksvåg, Peder Tobiassen, 57

famine: reason for emigration, 9

Finnmark region, Norway, 105

Flagstad, Kirsten, 104

folk music, 61, 69, 72, 81–82, 84

Ford, Henry, 53

Ford, Mrs. Henry, 106

Ford Motor Car Co., 22, 53

Frankfort, MI, 20–21; hospital at, 64–65;
newspaper at, 59–60

Frederickson, Charles, 20–21

freethinking, 143 (n. 80)

Frimodig, David, 59

Frimodig, Isaac, 58

G

General Motors, 55–56

Giants in the Earth, 14

Gjelsness, Rudolph, 62–63, 65

Grand Haven, MI, 14–15, 18

Grand Rapids, MI: furniture industry
at, 37

Grand Rapids Bridge Company, 52

Grieg, Edvard, 83–84, 96

Guthrie, Woody: ballad by, 42

H

Haakon the Good, King, 109

Haakon VII, King, 106

Håkon Håkonsson, Prince, 47

Hansen, H. C., 19

Hanson, Harry B., 54

Harbor Beach, MI, 19

Hardanger fiddle, 69, 80–82, 98

Hauge, Hans Nielsen, 69–70

Helgeby, Ralph O., 55–56

Hemingway, Ernest: feature story about,
60

Henry Ford II (ore boat), 22

Hexagon Tool and Engineering Co., 54

"Hils fra meg der hjemme," 22–23, 25

Hoff, Carl and Olga, 104–105

Hoff, Olaf, 52

Holman, Hans-Jørgen, 61, 81

Holter, Aksel, 49

hospitals, 63–64

huldre folk, 96–97, 112, 114

I

Illinois, 32

Ingebritson, Pearl, 111

Ireland, 5, 7

Iron Mountain, MI, 45

Ironwood, MI, 45

Irving Gilmore International Piano
Festival, 84

Ishpeming, MI, 45, 57, 59; Lutheran
church at, 45; ski club at, 47–48;
Suicide Hill at, 50

Isle Royale, MI, 22–25

J

Jackson, Ena, 64

"Jeg er så glad kver julekveld" (Christmas carol), 113

Jensen, Halvor, 18

Johnson, Holger and Lucy, 24–25

Johnson, John, 35

Johnson, O. A., 22

Jolstad, Trygve, 53

julenissen, 109–10, 112

K

Kahn, Albert, 54

Kalamazoo, MI, 61, 84

Keillor, Garrison, 80

Keweenaw Peninsula, MI, 41

Kjerulf, Halfdan, 83

knitting, 90

Kyrkjebø, Sissel, 84

L

LaBianca, Øystein S., 61

Lake Erie, 13

Lake Huron, 19

Lake Michigan, 10; ferry service, 13–15,
17, 20, 32

Lake Superior, 22–23

langeleik (stringed instrument), 80

language: Norwegian, 10–11, 35, 48, 71, 75, 113, 122, 145 (n. 118)

Lansing, MI: seat of state government at, 58

Larson, Alexander, 21

Larson, LeRoy, 79–80, 98

LaRue, Frank, 63–64

Letters from America, 7

Lindeman, Ludvig, 72, 125–126

Linderup (steam tug), 18

Lutheran Hymnary, 72–73, 125–26

Lysne, Per, 91

M

Maakestad, John, 35

Manistee, MI, 17–18; river basin, 37

Manistique, MI, 21

Marquette, MI, 90: County Historical Museum at, 59; General Hospital at, 63; iron range at, 45–46

Melitta (schooner), 18–19

Melkeld family, 32–33, 35; Inga, 32; Ivor, 32; Martin, 32

Menominee: iron range at, 46

Midsummer, 80

Milwaukee, WI, 32, 37

Minneapolis, MN: center of Scandinavian popular music, 79; school of painting, 91

Minnesota, 17, 23, 28, 46, 49

Moss, Norway, 7

Muskegon, MI, 38–40, 115; Dynamite Saloon at, 39; Lutheran churches at, 67, 69–70

"My Heart is Longing to Praise My Savior" (folk hymn), 126–127

N

National Ski Association, 49, 57

National Ski Hall of Fame, 49, 59

"Nikolina," 23

nisser (fairy creatures), 98, 114

Norden Ski Club, 48

Northport, MI: Lutheran church at, 67–68, 86

Norwegian American Women's Club, 106, 115

"Norwegian Dance" (from *Norwegian Peasant Dances*), 83

Norwegian Folk Museum (on Bygdøy, at Oslo), 22

Norwegian Men's Club, 115

Norwegian Royal University Chorus, 83

Nystedt, Knut, 84

O

Olaf Haroldson, Saint and King, 75–77, 95

Olaf Trygvason, King, 47, 83

Oleson, John, 17

Olsen, N. H. N., 53–54

Olsen, Nils Andreas: of Bjorn family, 58

Osceola Mine, 58

P

painting: by Norwegian artists, 44–45, 86, 90–91. *See also* rosemaling

Peterson, Arthur, 64–65

Peterson, Isaac, 118

Peterson, John E., 60

Peterson, Pete, 59

Peterson, Peter (farmer), 28–29

Peterson, Peter (lighthouse keeper), 19

Pierson, Harriet, 10

population: increase in Norway, 8

Port Huron, MI: railroad tunnel at, 52

psalmodikon, 145 (n. 110)

Q

Quebec: transit point, 14, 42

Quincy Mine, 58

Quisling, Vidkun, 104, 130

R

Råde, Norway: church at, 8, 122

railroads, 10, 14–15, 51; narrow gauge, 38

Reissiger, F. A., 83

Restauration (sloop), 1, 17

Riser, Knud Sophus, 52

River Rouge factory, 54

Rokicki, Susan, 57

Røldal: crucifix at, 85

Rollo the Northman, 7

Rølvaag, O. E., 10, 14, 71

Roosevelt, Theodore, 49

Rornas, Hans Christian, 43

rosemaling, 90–92

S

Saginaw River: bridge over, 52

Sandefjord Girl's Choir, 84

Sandman, Jeff, 60

Sandman, Peter, 59

Sangdahl, L. E., 52

Sault St. Marie, MI, 18

Scandinavian Symphony (of Detroit), 84

Scarvie, Walter B., 106–107

Scotland, 5–7

Seglem, Elling, 24

Selden, Margery Stomne, 60

Setesdal region, Norway: sweaters from, 89

Simonson, Dorothy, 24

Sinding, Christian, 83

Singstad, Ole, 52

Sivertson, Howard, 24

Skandinaven (newpaper), 51

Snorre Sel (children's book), 129

Soli, Herman, 85

sølje (silver brooch), 88–89

Sommers, Lawrence M., 60–61

Sons of Norway, 88, 115, 123

Stokker, Kathleen, 100

Stony Creek, MI, 15

Stordahl, Peder Ludvig, 57

Stordahl, Wayne, 57

Stromsing, Peter, 98

Strong, Grace, 90–91

Stubhaug, Ole Mathias, 15

Sturlason, Snorre, 47, 76

"The Sun Has Gone Down" (religious folksong), 126

Sweden, 100, 107

Syttende Mai (Norwegian Constitution Day), 22, 24, 80, 100

T

Taftezon, Christian, 42

Tall Hisban (archaeological site in Jordan), 61

Taylor, Frederick Winslow, 55

Tellefsen, Carl, 49

Terboven, Joseph, 104

Their Father's God, 71

Thoen, Inger, 103, 105, 129–130

Thoresen, Soren A., 52

Tord Gustavsen Trio, 84

trolls, 95–97, 112, 114, 145 (n. 111)

U

Ulseth, Edward, 43, 57

U.P. Engineering and Architectural
    Associates, 57

V

Vesterheim Museum, 86, 93

vestments: for clergy, 86–87

Vikings, 1, 5–7, 93

Virch, Pat, 93

W

Wagbo, Martha, 34–35

Wagbo, Olga: family history by, 34

wall paintings, 45, 90–91

Wemmerlund, E. K., 55

William the Conqueror, 6–7

Willow Run Airport, 54

Winyah (steamer), 23

Wisconsin, 32

witches, kitchen, 99

women: role of, 35

World War II, 56, 103–107, 129–30

Y

York, 6–7, 77